BRAZIL
1954-64:
End of a
Civilian Cycle

INTERIM
HISTORY

BRAZIL
1954-64:
End of a
Civilian Cycle

Edited by Jordan M. Young
Professor of History
Pace College (New York)

FACTS ON FILE, INC.   NEW YORK

BRAZIL
1954-64:
End of a
Civilian Cycle

Library of Congress Catalog Card No. 73-184921

ISBN 0-87196-214-4

9 8 7 6 5 4 3 2 1

PRINTED IN THE UNITED STATES OF AMERICA

CONTENTS

i

1959

1960

1961

1962

1963

1964

INTRODUCTION

GETULIO VARGAS, THE BRAZILIAN ex-dictator who returned to power by winning a valid presidential election, put a bullet through his heart in mid-1954 when, for the 2d time, the military decided to force him out of office. Somewhat less than 10 years later Vargas' former protege Joao Goulart was also removed from the presidency by Brazil's military leaders. This book records the events that took place in Brazil in the interval between these changes of administration.

The years 1954-64 were a decade of both promise and disappointment for Brazil. Magnificent new economic programs were proposed and inaugurated, but progress lagged. The country's capital was moved from the Atlantic coast to a grand new city created in Brazil's interior as a symbol of the nation's determination to open up and develop its unused heartland. The transfer of locale did change old attitudes and spur Brazilians to new effort. Brazilian leaders joined in dreaming of and planning a hemispherewide economic-social alliance designed to bring prosperity, health and education to all the backward areas of Latin America, but early results were disappointing.

Brazil, more than any other Western Hemisphere nation, brings to mind the story of the blind men as they all touched different parts of an elephant and described the animal in terms of the part they touched. Similarly, all who have researched, studied, wondered and wandered over this incredible Brazil have come away with a different image. What this volume attempts is to record important facts about Brazil during a critical period and to bring them into focus.

Brazil in 1954 had about 57 million people. A decade later there were perhaps 78,800,000 Brazilians. These numbers, of course, are only rough estimates. Even the census, which was

1

POPULATION & AREA OF BRAZIL'S STATES, TERRITORIES & REGIONS

(Population as of 1960 census)

State or territory	Area in square kilometers	Percent of national area	Population	Percent of national population
North				
Rondônia *	243,044	2.86	70,783	0.10
Acre	152,589	1.79	160,208	0.23
Amazonas	1,558,987	18.38	721,215	1.02
Roraima *	230,104	2.70	29,489	0.04
Pará	1,227,530	14.66	1,550,935	2.18
Amapá *	139,068	1.65	68,889	0.10
Northeast				
Maranhão	324,616	3.86	2,492,139	3.51
Piauí	250,934	2.95	1,263,368	1.78
Ceará	148,016	1.74	3,337,856	4.70
Rio Grande do Norte	53,015	0.62	1,157,258	1.63
Paraíba	56,372	0.66	2,018,023	2.84
Pernambuco	98,281	1.16	4,136,900	5.83
Alagôas	27,652	0.33	1,127,062	1.80
Southeast				
Sergipe	21,994	0.26	760,273	1.07
Bahia	559,921	6.59	5,990.605	8.44
Minas Gerais	583,248	6.85	9,798,880	13.81
Espirito Santo	39,368	0.46	1,188,665	1.80
Serra dos Aimorés †	10,153	0.12	384,297	0.54
Rio de Janeiro	42,134	0.50	3,402,728	4.80
Guanabara	1,356	0.02	3,307,163	4.66
South				
São Paulo	247,898	2.91	12,974,699	18.28
Paraná	199,060	2.64	4,277,763	6.03
Santa Catarina	95,483	1.13	2,146,909	3.03
Rio Grande do Sul	267,528	3.32	5,448,823	7.67
Central-West				
Mato Grosso	1,213,549	14.47	910,262	1.28
Goiás	642,036	7.54	1,954,862	2.76
Federal District	5,814	0.07	141,742	0.20
Total	8,511,965	100.00	70,967,185	100.00

REGIONAL SUMMARY

North	3,551,322	42.17	2,601,519	3.67
Northeast	985,912	11.32	15,677,995	22.09
East	1,257,989	14.80	24,832,611	34.99
South	809,060	9.70	24,848,194	35.01
Central-West	1,861,399	22.04	3,006,866	4.24

* Territory.
† The Serra does Aimorés area was claimed by the states of Minas Gerais and Espirito Santo.

taken in 1950 and 1960*, produced data generally regarded as guesses. But one could sense the stirring of a giant in those years, although Brazilians then—and Brazilians today—do not know exactly what is inside their country.

The political development of this Portuguese-speaking nation has been consistently different from that of the other Latin American countries. Since its discovery in 1500 by Pedro Alvares Cabral, a Portuguese admiral sailing in theory toward India, Brazil's social, political and economic march has been to a unique cadence. Neglected by Portugal, Brazil in a sense gained its independence long before the colony officially broke its bonds with the mother country in the 19th century. Although they had been beset by many foreign invaders, it was the 1630 Dutch occupation of nearly 1,200 square miles of the northeastern coastal area that provoked the Brazilians into action. Portugal seemed less concerned with the loss of national territory, and thus the Brazilians took on the task themselves. Nationalism developed early for Brazilians as a result of their expulsion of the Dutch invaders in 1654.

Brazil's relationship to Africa was unique. The sugar-cane economy depended on a steady supply of slaves from Africa. Some historians suggest that the African colony of Angola was perhaps more a colony of Brazil than it was of Portugal; more often than not Brazilian administrators went from Brazil to Angola to run the African colony. Brazilians recognize and pay tribute to their African heritage. The impact of Africa appears in the music, food, language, religion and color of Brazil's citizens.

The racial mix of Brazil does not mean that Brazilians are free of racial prejudice. Such prejudice does exist there, but as Carl Degler pointed out in *Neither Black Nor White,* in Brazil there is little racial discrimination.

When King Joao VI of Portugal fled from Napoleon in 1808 and took refuge in Brazil, his presence knocked Brazilian historical development out of joint. Joao VI raised the colony of Brazil to equal kingdom status with Portugal in 1816. This magnified status gave Brazilians a sense of being a big and important nation, and this has remained the hallmark of their approach to world problems. But perhaps of equal importance

---

* According to the census, Brazil's population rose from 51,976,357 July 1, 1950 to 70,967,185 Sept. 1, 1960.

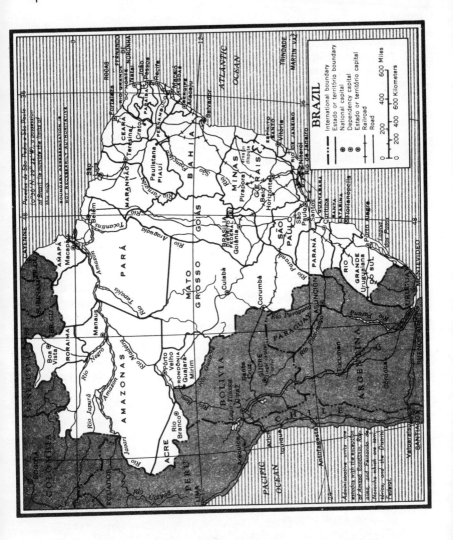

was the fact that the Portuguese royal house of Braganca, while in Brazil during 1808-21, established professional military, naval, scientific and botanical institutes that provided an infra-structure lacking in other Latin American countries.

Joao VI returned to Portugal in 1821, and Brazil gained independence in 1822, easily and with little violence. Portugal did not fight to retain Brazil when Pedro, the son of the Portuguese king, declared Brazil free and independent and assumed the title of Dom Pedro I, emperor of Brazil. His reign lasted from 1822 to 1831.

A monarchy in the New World! Strange, exotic, yet somehow, historians say, it worked in Brazil for quite awhile. Ultimately, however, Brazilians began to describe Dom Pedro I as too imperial. They complained that he squandered public funds, lost the territory of Uruguay and meddled in Portuguese politics. Dom Pedro was forced to abdicate in 1831. No violence attended this change in government, and Pedro left his young Brazilian-born son, Pedro II, as heir to the throne, while a regency of wealthy landowners and clerics governed the country until 1841.

Brazil was ruled by Pedro II from 1841 to 1889. During this period the country was relatively stable, though stagnant, while most of Latin America went through cycles of *caudillos,* wars and revolutions. Although Brazil enjoyed political stability, the country suffered repeated economic cycles: from wood to sugar, from sugar to gold, from gold back to sugar and then to rubber and finally to coffee. Each economic boom made a different part of the country wealthier and brought more people into the economic and social network of the nation. Yet when Emperor Pedro II fell in 1889, Brazil, basically, was still a tightly run oligarchy with a mere fraction of the population involved in the political and economic processes.

Shifting political and economic currents caused the collapse of the empire. The downfall of the powerful landowners of the northeast came when slavery was abolished May 13, 1888. May 13 is a national holiday, but it sounded the death knell of the monarchy. Without the support of the land-holding oligarchy, Dom Pedro II had few options open. The Church had been alienated by Pedro's determination to dominate the religious structure of his country, and the Brazilian Catholic Church therefore did little to support the aging monarch. The rising military class, basically a middle-class group, lost confidence in the emperor and ousted him in Nov. 1889 without bloodshed.

Republican Brazil lasted from 1889 to 1930. The new Republican politicians were in large part the former monarchists who simply shifted their allegiance to the new republican form of government. A new constitution prepared in 1891 set up the traditional 3 branches of government—the executive, the legislative and the judiciary. In Brazil, as in many other Latin American countries, the executive branch of the government was far more powerful than the other 2. Brazilian presidents were usually supported by the military, although there were unsuccessful military revolts in 1922 and 1924. Rarely did a Brazilian president place himself in the position of opposing army demands. What some historians find curious is how modest and undemanding the Brazilian military were in the period 1889-1930.

Chief executives, with rare exceptions, represented the economic, political and social interests of the 2 most powerful states of the union, Minas Gerais and Sao Paulo. Presidents were elected every 4 years on schedule. Congressmen and senators ran for office and performed their duties until the system fell apart in 1930. In that year economic crisis combined with a challenge from a newly emerging state, Rio Grande do Sul, to give the Brazilian military cause to withdraw their support from the old system.

A contested presidential election in 1930, in which Getulio Dornelles Vargas, governor of Rio Grande do Sul, was pitted against Gov. Julio Prestes of Sao Paulo, provided the agitated political milieu for the downfall of the "old republic." Vargas lost the election, but he was able to take advantage of a skillfully planned military *coup d'etat* that, in Oct. 1930, swept him into power. Much of the military success was due to planning and preparation by Lt. Col. Goes Monteiro and rebel officers from the unsuccessful 1922 and 1924 revolutions. Following the Brazilian pattern, there was little or no bloodshed during the events of Oct. 1930. Vargas dominated Brazil as provisional president 1930-3, as elected president 1934-7 and as dictator 1937-45. Vargas left office Oct. 29, 1945 when the Brazilian military lost confidence in him.

The 15 Vargas years were important ones for Brazil. The economic depression resulted in a shift in economic activity. The coffee barons of Sao Paulo were forced to divert funds from land into a growing industrial plant because Brazil did not have the dollars necessary to import manufactured goods. The Vargas government also brought the labor movement into the body politic without the wrenching struggles that occurred in Argentina and Mexico. A small middle class developed during the Vargas years. On the political level the 15-year Vargas period was one of authoritarian rule with little freedom permitted or encouraged. Yet Brazil prospered economically. Of course, it was said, those close to the Vargas team prospered most of all. It was also said that the failure to provide political experience for Brazilians during the Vargas period had cost the nation dearly in the next 19 years. Strange political alliances and abuses by charismatic leaders were part of the legacy left by the authoritarian years of Vargas. The wealthy states of Brazil, Sao Paulo, Minas Gerais and then Rio Grande do Sul to some extent coupled voter strength with economic power.

Early in 1945, when it had become evident that the Allies were going to win World War II, pressure had built up for Vargas to restore democratic government. Carlos Lacerda, a crusading newspaperman, broke the censorship. Then political parties began to form.

Brazil had participated in World War II on the Allied side. The country entered the war in Aug. 1942 after German marines sank 5 Brazilian merchant ships. By taking part in the war, Brazil received a great deal of U.S. military hardware and, even more important, a U.S.-financed modern steel mill that gave further help to Brazil's industrial infra-structure. By 1945, when Getulio Vargas was forced to leave office, the nation was well on the way to modernization. 15 years of dictatorship had centralized Brazil in the sense that communications were improved and regional differences somewhat blurred. A relatively strong national government with a desire to put its imprint on all of Brazil resulted in the breaking or weakening of the power of some of the local oligarchies.

Vargas was supported during almost all his years in power by the Brazilian army. Merit-oriented, the military continued to represent the middle class and not the elite land-owning families. The army was and is a means of social and economic ladder-climbing. It was heavily staffed with people from the poverty-stricken northeast and military-oriented citizens of the southern state of Rio Grande do Sul. Sophisticated, educated young men from the elite families of Sao Paulo and Minas Gerais did not enter the army. These young men turned rather to the industrial and financial world.

But the warm relationship between Getulio Vargas and the Brazilian military came to an end when it appeared in the closing months of 1945 that Vargas was building a new political power base dependent on the working class and perhaps excluding the military. Early in Oct. 1945 Juan and Evita Peron of Argentina mobilized the packing house workers in Buenos Aires to obtain Peron's release from jail. This example of the effectiveness of powerful labor support was not lost on Vargas—nor on the Brazilian military. When Vargas began to use government funds for demonstrations in Rio de Janeiro of workers demanding that Vargas remain in power, the army moved and deposed him Oct. 29, 1945. As usual in Brazil, there was no bloodshed or disorders.

Vargas retired to his ranch in Rio Grande do Sul near Sao Borja on the Uruguayan border, where one of the few constant visitors was a neighbor, a young rancher named Joao Goulart. The 2 men became close friends.

Brazil thus entered its 2d period of Republican government, which lasted from 1945 to 1964.

Presidential elections were held Dec. 2, 1945. The military had little to worry about since both of the major candidates were army men. The victor was Gen. Eurico Gaspar Dutra, selected earlier by the Vargas-organized Social Democratic Party (Partido Social Democratico, or PSD) and in part by a badly split Brazilian Labor Party (Partido Trabalhista Brasileiro, or PTB). The other major candidate was Air Force Brig. Eduardo Gomes, who had been nominated by a strong anti-Vargas coalition of middle-class elements controlling the National Democratic Union (Uniao Democratica Nacional, or UDN). There was a small flurry of excitement when the Brazilian Communist Party (PCB), which had been permitted to surface in Apr. 1945, named Yeddo Fiuza in November as its candidate for president.

Dutra won by a comfortable margin. The results were: Dutra (PSD), 3,250,000 votes, or 55%; Gomes (UDN), 2,040,000 votes, or 35%; Fiuza (PCB), 600,000 votes, or 10%.

In the Congressional elections Vargas was elected a senator from Rio Grande do Sul. The Congressional results: PSD, 151 seats, 42%; UDN, 77 seats, 26%; PTB, 22 seats, 10%; PCB, 14 seats, 9%.

The PSD represented the wealthy elements of the former Vargas team, and it remained in control of many of the smaller states of the Brazilian union. The Vargas-sponsored PTB was an attempt to draw on the loyalty of the newly developing working class and form it into a party that could be controlled. The UDN was composed basically of the middle class, which had opposed the Vargas government. The only other significant party among the many small political groupings was the PSP (Social Progressive Party, or Partido Social Progressista), which carried weight in Sao Paulo and a few northeastern states. The PSP was the personal vehicle of Sao Paulo politician Ademar de Barros, and it catered to the working class of Sao Paulo. Many *Paulistas* (residents of the state of Sao Paulo) acknowleged that de Barros stole money from the public, but they also held that he did useful things for the state. He was a popular figure, and his ability to mobilize voters in both Sao Paulo and the northeast gave him power and forced the major political parties and national politicians to pay attention to him.

Shortly after Dutra was inaugurated as president in Jan. 1946, the new Congress met as a Constituent Assembly, and in Sept. 1946 it approved a new constitution that served, with modifications, until the revolution of 1964.

Dutra carried into the presidency the same administrative talent and personality that he had demonstrated in the army. His style was bland non-commitment to any one position except that of anti-communism. As time passed he favored outlawing the Communist Party, which increased its strength in the Jan. 1947 mid-term elections. In May 1947 the Communist Party was declared illegal on the ground that it violated provisions of the 1946 constitution.

The economic situation that faced Dutra was excellent. Brazil's gold reserves were at a record high, but the government and the people went on a buying spree that quickly depleted the treasury and sapped the economy. Cars, refrigerators, luxury items of all types were imported in vast quantities. By the time the Dutra administration ended in 1950, more than $2 billion had been spent on imports. A vast black market developed in illegally imported goods, and graft reached great heights. The cruzeiro, Brazil's monetary unit, began to weaken, and an inflationary trend began.

Petroleum nationalism under the slogan *"O Petroleo e Nosso"* (the oil is ours) was born during the Dutra administration in the face of exploitation by foreign oil firms of Brazilian oil. A program of economic development, called the SALTE program, was presented in May 1948 in an effort to develop transportation, electrification, nutrition and public health, but Dutra never succeeded in overcoming Brazil's economic ills.

As the Dutra administration approached its close, the name of Getulio Vargas began to be mentioned as a possible candidate for the next presidential term. On his 67th birthday, Apr. 19, 1950, a Vargas birthday party at Joao Goulart's ranch was turned into a political rally, and Vargas' hat was officially in the ring. The PTB supported Vargas. A political deal was quickly made with Ademar de Barros, and the PSP also made his nomination official. Running with Vargas as vice presidential candidate was Joao Cafe Filho from Rio Grande do Norte. In May the PSD selected Cristiano Machado, a Minas Gerais politician, as its official presidential candidate. Altino Arantes won the vice presidential nomination. PSD voters, however, were still emotionally attached to Vargas. The UDN renominated Brig. Eduardo Gomes and named Odilon Braga for the vice presidency.

In the election Oct. 3, 1950, Vargas was chosen president. The results: Vargas, 3,849,040 votes; Gomes, 2,342,384 votes; Machado, 1,679,193 votes. Cafe Filho was elected vice president with 2,520,790 votes; Braga received 2,344,841 votes and Arantes 1,649,309.

Vargas, inaugurated in Jan. 1951, at first tried to assemble his old team from the years in which he had been dictator. Gen. Goes Monteiro, who had headed the military phase of the 1930 revolution and had worked closely with Vargas until Oct. 1945, was appointed head of the General Staff of the Armed Forces. As war minister, Vargas selected Maj. Gen. Newton Estillac Leal.

Vargas faced many problems, but economic woes and political chaos were the greatest. When Vargas had been dictator it had been a simple matter to direct economic policy and issue executive orders. But in the new political system, many agreements and "understandings" had to be reached before legislation would be passed by Congress. As result, there was no clear-cut government economic policy.

In the face of heavy pressure from nationalists in every sector of the Brazilian political spectrum, the Petrobras law (No. 2004) was passed Oct. 3, 1953, and a government monopoly was established over the search for petroleum and the development of the oil industry. But food prices continued to rise, and inflation plagued Brazil's salaried workers.

Vargas' greatest problems, however, were those that arose in the political arena. Irregularities in government operations were uncovered frequently. An example was the illicit financing (through the Banco do Brasil) of a newspaper in Rio de Janeiro, *Ultima Hora,* which published only information favorable to the administration.

The downfall and suicide of Vargas can be traced to a series of events that began June 15, 1953, the day Vargas nominated Joao Goulart as his new labor minister. Goulart, who replaced Jose Segadas Viana, apparently began to build a tight political organization based on the trade unions. Whenever a union went on strike, it appeared to have the support of the labor minister. A situation similar to that of Oct. 1945 began to develop. The military charged that Vargas was once again building a new power base. Military action was not long in coming, and a group of generals Oct. 16, 1953 signed a "memorial" charging Goulart with interference in the political life of the nation. The tempo of events increased as Goulart maintained pressure for higher wages for the workers. By Feb. 1954 dissension had spread to the lower-ranking officers, and 82 colonels and lieutenant colonels complained in a signed manifesto to the government about the wage increases to the workers while their own salaries lagged so far behind.

Goulart was forced to resign from the Vargas cabinet Feb. 22, 1954, and tension subsided temporarily, until the old feud between newspaperman Carlos Lacerda and Getulio Vargas brought down the Vargas administration and culminated in Vargas' suicide.

Vargas, born Apr. 19, 1883 in Sao Borja, Rio Grande do Sul, was the son of a local political leader who had served in the Paraguayan War and had earned the title of honorary general in the Brazilian army. Getulio Vargas also joined the army, in his teens, and served briefly in the 25th Infantry Battalion. He began practicing law in Porto Alegre at 24 and was named public prosecutor a year later. He was active in state politics in 1909-23, and he organized a division of troops to quell a local revolution. Vargas was named federal finance minister by Pres. Washington Luis Pereira de Souza in 1926, but he resigned a year later and became governor of his home state, Rio Grande do Sul. 4 years later he began his national career with his unsuccessful nomination as a presidential candidate in 1930. After the Vargas-led revolt, military leaders caused the collapse of the Washington Luis regime and gave Vargas unlimited power Oct. 24, 1930. After being elected president under the new constitution in 1934, Vargas established his dictatorship in 1937, suspended the constitution and abolished representative government. He supported the Allies during World War II. Vargas was deposed by army and navy leaders in Oct. 1945. In his later years, after again being elected president in 1950, he concentrated on industrialization and the development of Brazil's natural resources.

This book records events in Brazil from the suicide of Vargas to the downfall in Apr. 1964 of the regime headed by his protege Joao Goulart.

1954

THE FALL OF VARGAS

1954 is a watershed year in Brazilian history. Pres. Getulio Vargas' suicide Aug. 24 was a stunning and unexpected event. Vargas, a shrewd and pragmatic politician, had governed Brazil as dictator for 15 years (1930-45). He had been removed from office by the military in 1945 but had returned to power by winning an open and free election for the presidency in 1950; he was popular with the working class, and many middle-class citizens felt that he would give them the type of administration from which they, too, could benefit.

Vargas, inaugurated in Jan. 1951, had found it difficult to govern a country that had a free and critical press. He also discovered that the legislative branch was wary of a former dictator and often would not pass legislation that the chief executive thought the nation needed. Vargas gathered around him many of his former cronies from the dictatorship period. The Brazilian military made it clear that it watched his performance with growing suspicion.

In June 1953, Vargas had selected a friend and neighbor, Joao Goulart, a young and politically inexperienced rancher from the state of Rio Grande do Sul, to serve as labor minister. Minimum wages were quickly raised, and labor unions were encouraged to unify into one huge government-sponsored General Trade Confederation. Vargas and Goulart seemed to be traveling the same path as Juan Peron of Argentina, and the

13

military, therefore, demanded that the cabinet be reorganized and the labor minister fired. Goulart was accused in army circles of trying to build up a labor-union following that could control the country. Gen. Ciro de Espirito Santo was forced by Vargas to resign as war minister because he supported a report by 82 army colonels warning of dissatisfaction in army ranks and criticizing high living costs and labor strikes in Brazil. The cabinet crisis was resolved Feb. 22, 1954 when Vargas appointed Gen. Euclides Zenobio da Costa as war minister and accepted Goulart's resignation.

Major Court Decisions

Despite these changes in the Vargas government, the Supreme Court July 5 upheld Vargas' decree under a new law that legal minimum wages in Brazil be doubled—to about $45 a month in Rio de Janeiro and to correspondingly equal levels elsewhere in the country.

Although army pressure on Communist activity continued, a special military court in Rio de Janeiro July 8 acquitted 44 persons accused of pro-Communist subversive activity in the armed forces. Documentation of a Communist action program for Brazil had been reported seized July 6 when Armilio de Vasconcelos, Communist ex-member of the Rio City Council and in hiding for 3 years, was arrested. 4 career diplomats suspended by Vargas in Mar. 1953 for alleged Communist sympathies won a reversal of the order in the Supreme Court July 10, 1954.

Attempt on Lacerda's Life

Tension mounted in August. Carlos Lacerda, editor of the *Tribuna da Imprensa* of Rio de Janeiro and an influential anti-administration voice, was shot and wounded, and Maj. Rubens Florentino Vaz, a companion, was shot and killed Aug. 5 in Rio by an assassin who apparently intended to kill Lacerda. Members of Vargas' personal bodyguard were accused of the shooting, and Vargas disbanded the bodyguard Aug. 9, assigning military police to the bodyguard function. Opponents in Congress demanded Vargas' resignation Aug. 10 because his administration had failed to apprehend Lacerda's assailant. Rio police used tear gas Aug. 11 to disperse anti-Vargas demonstrators who had started a riot outside the headquarters of Vargas' Labor Party.

The tempo of events continued to accelerate as the air force's military police went on a manhunt for Vaz' killer. The climax came when an ex-presidential bodyguard, Climerio Euribes de Almeida, was arrested by the air force Aug. 17. He was charged as the mastermind of the attack on Vaz and Lacerda. Earlier, the air force had arrested the alleged gunman, who was reported to have confessed that he had slain Vaz and to have declared that Deputy Lutero Vargas, son of Pres. Vargas, had ordered Lacerda's assassination. Lutero Vargas denied this Aug. 13.

Lutero Vargas and other government figures were cleared Aug. 14 by an air force investigation of implication in the slaying. It was established that, without Vargas' knowledge, the chief of the presidential guard, Gregorio Fortunato, had given the orders and had paid for the murder. The killer was identified as Alcino Joao do Nascimento.

Generals' Manifesto Demands Vargas Quit

The military continued their pressure on Vargas, and more than 30 generals Aug. 23 signed a manifesto demanding that the president resign. *Text of the manifesto:*

Manifesto to the nation:

Considering that the military police inquiry taking place at the Galeao Airbase has already clearly ascertained that it was the personal guard of the president of the republic, under the orders of Gregorio Fortunato (a man trusted completely by the president), who planned and prepared within the Presidential Palace and ordered the carrying out of the attempt which resulted in the assassination of air force Maj. Ruben Florentino Vaz.

Considering that [although] the president of the republic had assured the nation that the crime would be investigated and the guilty ones brought to trial, people of his immediate confidence, within the Presidential Palace, warned the criminals and provided the means, including vast quantities of money, enabling them to flee.

Considering that it is extremely doubtful that all the guilty ones will be punished:

Considering that the inquiry has brought to light ample criminal corruption in circles closest to the president of the republic:

Considering that these facts compromise the moral authority that is indispensable for the president of the republic to exercise his mandate:

Considering finally that the extended actual political crisis is causing the country irremedial damages in the economic area and could possibly end in serious internal commotions, in view of the general uneasiness and repulsion that is encountered in all social classes of the country:

The signatories below, generals of the army, conscious of their duties and responsibilities before the nation—honoring their appointments, which were publicly and freely assumed—joining with the thoughts of their comrades in the air force and the navy, feel that the best path to calm the people and maintain the armed forces united is the resignation of the president of the republic [and] arranging his substitution in accord with the dictates of the constitution.

Rio 22 Aug. 1954.

[Signed] Gen. Alvaro Fiuza de Castro, Gen. Canrober Pereira da Costa, Gen. Nicanor Guimaraes de Souza, Gen. Juarez Tavora, Gen. Alcides G. Etchegoyen, Gen. Emilo R. Ribas Jor., Gen. Edgar Amaral, Gen. Altair de Queiroz, Gen. J. Machado Lopes, Gen. Peri Constant Bevilacqua, Gen. Humberto Castelo Branco, Gen. Paulo Kruger da Cunha Cruz, Gen. Ignacio Jose Verissimo, Gen. Barros Falcao, Gen. Joao Batista Rangel, Gen. Nilo Horacio de Oliveira Sucupira, Gen. Antonio Coelho dos Reis, Gen. Delso Fonseca, Gen. Henrique Lott, Gen. Otavio Saldanha Mazza, Gen. Jose Daudt Fabricio, Gen. Nestor Souto de Oliveira, Gen. Nilo August Guerreiro Lima, Gen. Penha Brasil, Gen. Jair Dantas Ribeiro.

Vargas Commits Suicide

Pres. Getulio Vargas, 71, agreed at about 4 a.m. Aug. 24 to take a leave of absence from the executive office in acquiescence to military pressure. $4\frac{1}{2}$ hours later he committed suicide by shooting himself through the heart.

Vargas at first had refused to resign. He had said Aug. 23 that he would not leave the presidency before the end of his term (Jan. 1, 1956) unless he were dead. But at an emergency cabinet meeting early Aug. 24, Vargas agreed to take a 90-day "leave of absence" and to turn over power to the vice president. A few hours later he killed himself.

Vargas left 2 notes. One, handwritten, declared: "To the wrath of my enemies I leave the legacy of my death. I carry with me the sorrow of not having been able to do for the humble all that I desired. Getulio Vargas." The 2d was a typewritten political manifesto that has become an important political document in Brazil. The text of the 2d letter:

Once more the forces and interests who are against the people are again coordinated and have broken loose against me.

They do not accuse me, they insult me; they do not fight me, they slander me and do not give me the right of defense. They need to drown my voice and halt my actions so that I no longer continue to defend, as I always have defended, the people and principally the humble.

I follow the destiny that is imposed on me. After decades of domination and looting by international economic and financial groups, I made myself head of a revolution and won. I began the work of liberation and I instituted a regime of social liberty. I had to resign. I returned to govern on the arms of the people.

A subterranean campaign of international groups joined with national groups revolting against the regime of workers' guarantees. The law of excess profits was stopped in Congress. Against the justice of a revision of minimum salaries, hatreds were unleashed.

I wished to create national liberty by developing our riches through Petrobras*, and no sooner had we begun when a wave of agitation was raised. Electrobrast† was hindered almost to despair. They do not wish the workers to be free. They do not wish the people to be independent.

I assumed the government during an inflationary spiral that was destroying the value of work. Profits of foreign enterprises reached 500 per cent yearly. In declaration of goods that we import there existed frauds of more than $100 million yearly.

The coffee crisis came, and increased the value of our principal product. We attempted to defend this price and the reply was a violent pressure upon our economy to the point of being obligated to surrender.

I have fought month to month, day to day, hour to hour, resisting constant aggression, unceasingly bearing it all in silence, forgetting all and renouncing myself to defend the people that now fall abandoned. I cannot give you more than my blood. If the birds of prey wish the blood of anybody, they wish to continue sucking that of the Brazilian people.

I offer my life in the holocaust. I choose this means to be with you always. When they humiliate you, you will feel my soul suffering at your side. When hunger beats at your door, you will feel in your chests the energy for the fight for yourselves and your children. When they humiliate you, you will feel my thoughts and this will give you strength to react.

My sacrifice will maintain you united, and my name will be your battle flag. Each drop of my blood will be an immortal call to your conscience and will maintain a sacred vibration for resistance.

To hatred, I respond with pardon. And to those who think they have defeated me, I reply with victory. I was the slave of the people and today I free myself for eternal life. But this people to which I was a slave no longer will be a slave to anyone. My sacrifice will remain forever in your soul and my blood will be the price of your ransom.

I fought against the looting of Brazil. I fought against the looting of the people. I have fought barebreasted. The hatred, infamy and calumny did not beat down my spirit. I gave you my life—now I offer you my death. Nothing remains. I have no fear. Serenely I take the first step on my road to eternity and I leave life to enter history.

—Getulio Vargas

---

* A government monopoly responsible for the development and production of petroleum products.
† An analogous organization responsible for the generation and distribution of electricity.

Public disturbances followed Vargas' suicide. 4 people were shot to death and several others were hurt Aug. 24-25 in riots after Vargas' death was announced. Many demonstrations, believed Communist-inspired, were aimed at U.S. property.

Vargas' body was flown Aug. 25 to his home in Rio Grande do Sul State for burial.

Cafe Filho Succeeds Vargas as President

Vice Pres. Joao Cafe Filho succeeded Vargas as president Aug. 24.

Cafe Filho had been born Feb. 3, 1899 in Natal, Rio Grande do Norte (he died Feb. 20, 1970). The son of a civil servant, Cafe Filho was a crusading journalist who had started his newspaper career at 19 by editing the *Gazeta* of Natal. He later founded the antigovernment *Jornal do Norte.* After this newspaper was suppressed in 1926, he fled to Bezerros in Pernambuco and started a newspaper there. He edited another opposition paper in Recife in 1928 and was jailed for attacking the state government. Cafe Filho joined the pro-Vargas Liberal Alliance in 1929 and commanded army forces in Natal in the 1930 revolution that put Vargas in power. He became chief of police under the military government, was later elected to Congress (in 1934) and served until Vargas dissolved the Congress in 1937. Because of his open opposition to the Vargas dictatorship he was exiled to Argentina. He returned to Brazil a year later but did not take part in politics until after Vargas' fall as dictator. Cafe Filho won election to Congress again in 1945 and achieved national attention for his investigations of government agencies. He led the Social Progressive Party in the northeast in an alliance with Vargas' Labor Party in the 1950 election and was inaugurated as vice president in 1951. He served all but the last 3 months of the remainder of Vargas' term of office.

Since presidential elections were scheduled for autumn 1955, Cafe Filho put together a stopgap cabinet filled with anti-Vargas politicians. The composition of the new cabinet, as announced Sept. 1: Dr. Raul Fernandes, foreign affairs; Prof. Eugenio Gudin, finance; Dr. Miguel Seabra Fagundes, justice; Col. Napoleao de Alencastro Guimaraes, labor; Jose Costa Porto, agriculture; Dr. Aramys Athayade, health; Prof. Candido Mota Filho, education; Gen. Henrique Baptista

Duffles Teixeira Lott, war; Adm. Edmundo Jordao Amorin do Valle, navy; Brig. Eduardo Gomes, air force; and Lucas Lopes, transport.

General Elections

Elections were held Oct. 3 for a new federal Chamber of Deputies, for 2/3 of the Senate and for the governorships of 11 of Brazil's 19 states and 3 territories. The elections evidenced a shift toward the center and conservative parties and away from the pro-Vargas alliance. In the lower house, Pres. Cafe Filho's source of support, the center parties, won more than 170 of the 324 seats. Of the 42 contested Senate seats, the Brazilian Labor Party (PTB) won fewer than 10. In Sao Paulo State, Mayor Janio Quadros of the capital city of Sao Paulo unseated the incumbent Ademar de Barros as governor. The Congressional results:

	Deputies	Senators
Social Democratic (PSD)	114	22
National Democratic (UDN)	74	13
Brazilian Labor (PTB)	56	16
Progressive Socialist (PSP)	36	4
Republican (PR)	16	4
Liberation (PL)	10	2
National Labor (PTN)	7	0
Christian Democratic (PDC)	2	0
Popular Representation (PRP)	5	0
Brazilian Socialist (PSB)	3	1
Social Workers' (PST)	1	1
Republican Workers' (PRT)	0	0
No party	0	1

Frost Damages Coffee Crop

One of the worst frosts in Brazilian history had occurred in Jan. 1953. The damage, which cut Brazil's coffee production by 1/3, did not have its full impact until nearly a year later in Dec. 1953, when the New York coffee market began to adjust to the shortage of Brazilian coffee. Santos 4 coffee prices began to rise for wholesalers, and by Aug. 1954 consumers in the U.S. were paying an unprecedented $1.23 a pound for coffee. The exports for the year 1954 were recorded at a low 10,918,000 bags worth approximately $24,800,000. In the previous year, 1953, Brazil had exported 15,562,000 bags valued at $21,696,000.

1955

PRESIDENTIAL ELECTION YEAR

1955 was another critical year for Brazil. The Cafe Filho administration managed to hold prices and wages in line but made no attempt to win popularity from the electorate. Relatively honest and free elections were held for the presidency in October, and the pro-Vargas slate of Juscelino Kubitschek and Joao Goulart won. The events of the following month, after Pres. Joao Cafe Filho suffered a heart attack, may never be described precisely and accurately enough to satisfy everyone.

Brazil had 2 military coups d'etat in November—the first when Gen. Henrique Lott forced Acting Pres. Carlos Luz out of office, the 2d when an ailing Pres. Cafe Filho left the hospital and said he was prepared to resume office. Lott moved again, and troops filled the streets of Rio de Janeiro. Congress, impressed with the show of military force, voted not to permit Cafe Filho to serve. Acting Senate Pres. Nereu Ramos was directed by Congress to act as chief executive until Kubitschek was inaugurated in 1956.

Presidential Election Maneuvers

Political maneuvering for the scheduled October presidential elections began as early as Jan. 28 when Transport Min. Lucas Lopes resigned from the cabinet to support Gov. Juscelino Kubitschek de Oliveira of Minas Gerais State as a candidate for president. Most Social Democratic Party (PSD) leaders favored Kubitschek, but Pres. Cafe Filho and army leaders demanded that Brazilian parties settle on a "National Union" candidate.

In February the PSD disregarded these pleas and officially nominated Kubitschek as its presidential candidate. The Popular Representation Party (PRP) Mar. 21 selected Plinio Salgado, former chief of the fascist Integralista party of the 1930s, as its presidential candidate. Conservative dissident Social Democrats Apr. 8 named Etelvino Lins, 47, ex-governor of Pernambuco State, to run for president.

Finance Min. Eugenio Gudin and Communications Min. Rodrigo Octavio Jordao Ramos resigned Apr. 5 after Pres. Cafe Filho agreed to let Sao Paulo Gov. Janio da Silva Quadros name new finance and communications ministers in return for cooperation in the elections. Justice Min. Alexandre Marcondes Filho resigned Apr. 12, reportedly for personal reasons. Cafe Filho took on 4 new cabinet members in April and May: Finance Min. Jose Maria Whitaker, 66, advocate of high coffee prices, named Apr. 9; Communications Min. Octavio Marcondes Ferraz, Apr. 14; Justice Min. J. E. Prado Kelly, Apr. 18, and Agriculture Min. Bento Munhoz da Rocha, May 2.

Maj. Gen. Newton Estillac Leal, 61, ex-war minister and army inspector general, died May 1, just after being named the presidential candidate of the Brazilian National Front (a leftist-nationalist coalition). Later in May, Sao Paulo's political boss, Ademar de Barros, won the presidential nomination of the Social Progressive Party (PSP).

The battle lines were clearly drawn in June: The National Democratic Union (UDN) selected Gen. Juarez Tavora as its candidate for the presidency; Etelvino Lins withdrew from the race, and ex-Labor Min. Joao Goulart agreed to run for the vice presidency on the Kubitschek ticket, thus forming a Brazilian Labor Party (PTB)-PSD alliance.

The Senate Sept. 2 rejected a proposal that the Chamber of Deputies decide the presidential election if none of the 4 candidates—Kubitschek, Tavora, de Barros or Salgado—received an absolute popular-vote majority. (A proposal that European-style parliamentary responsibility for government be adopted in place of Brazil's current U.S.-patterned administration failed to win the necessary $2/3$ support in the Chamber Sept. 2

although favored by a vote of 124-86. Pres. Cafe Filho's indorsement of a plan to move the Brazilian national capital from Rio de Janeiro to an unoccupied site of 300 square miles in southeastern Goiaz State, near the geographical center of the country, was announced Sept. 12. The new capital was later named Brasilia.)

Kubitschek Elected President

Juscelino Kubitschek de Oliveira, 54, of Czech descent, won the presidential election Oct. 3. Kubitschek's running mate, Joao (Jango) Goulart, 37, considered by many as Vargas' political heir, became vice president-elect. The vote for president:

Juscelino Kubitschek (PSD-PTB)	3,077,411	36%
Juárez Tavora (UDN)	2,610,462	30%
Adémar de Barros (PSP)	2,222,725	26%
Plínio Salgado (PRP)	632,848	8%

(Ademar de Barros, 55, ex-governor of Sao Paulo State, was convicted Mar. 6, 1956 of embezzling funds while governor. He was sentenced to 2 years in prison, fined 5,000 cruzeiros [$72] and deprived of his civil rights for 5 years.)

Voters were permitted to split their tickets and cast separate ballots for the vice-presidential candidates. As a result, Goulart and Milton Campos, the runner-up, each received more votes than the presidential victor, Kubitschek. The vice-presidential results:

João Goulart (PTB)	3,413,651	. . .
Milton Campos (UDN)	3,253,194	. . .
Danton Coelho (PSP)	1,127,907	. . .

Political Turmoil Follows Election

Pres.-elect Kubitschek was slated to take office Jan. 31, 1956 for a 5-year term when Joao Cafe Filho finished the term of the late Getulio Vargas.

But Cafe Filho's administration began to crumble shortly after the election. Jose M. Whitaker resigned as finance minister Oct. 10 after Cafe Filho refused to enact his foreign exchange reforms. Whitaker, a free-trade exponent, had sought to set up a single dollar-cruzeiro exchange rate for exporters of cotton, coffee and other products. These others resigned Oct. 10 in sympathy with Whitaker: Bank of Brazil Pres. Alcides da Costa Vidigal, Communications & Public Works Min.

Marcondes Ferraz, Brazilian Coffee Institute Pres. Raul Rocha
Medeiros. Mario Leopoldo Pereira da Camara, 64, was named
finance minister Oct. 11.

Political tension mounted when *Tribuna da Imprensa*'s
editor, Carlos Lacerda, in a blistering editorial, urged the
armed forces Oct. 14 to prevent the newly elected Kubitschek
from taking office as president. Provoked by the editorial, a
number of high-ranking army officers Oct. 15 issued a proclamation affirming the army's intention of upholding the
constitution against the possibility of a coup. Gen. Euclides
Zenobia da Costa, army inspector general, was dismissed by the
War Ministry Oct. 18 along with 2 other high-ranking officers,
Gen. Alcides Etchegoyen and Col. Alberto Bittencourt, for
taking part in politics by associating themselves with the
proclamation.

The 2 Coups d'Etat

Pres. Cafe Filho, who had suffered a heart attack, took an
indefinite leave of absence Nov. 8. As provided by the Brazilian
constitution, the speaker of the Chamber of Deputies, Carlos
Coimbra da Luz, 61, became acting president.

The war minister, Lt. Gen. Henrique Baptista Duffles
Teixeira Lott, demanded that the acting president discipline
Col. Jurandyr de Bizarra Mamede, commander of the Superior
War College, who had publicly urged a coup to cancel
Kubitschek's election as president. When Luz refused to act
against Mamede, Lott resigned Nov. 10 and was replaced as
war minister by Lt. Gen. Alvaro Fiuza de Castro.

But the following morning, early Nov. 11, Lott, reportedly
convinced that Luz was planning a coup to prevent Kubitschek
from taking office, staged what he (Lott) called a "preventive
coup," or countercoup. With the army following his orders,
Lott deposed Luz as acting president. Luz, Carlos Lacerda,
Mamede and various other political figures fled the country
aboard the naval cruiser *Tamandare* (the former *U.S.S. St.
Louis*). As the *Tamandare* steamed out of the harbor of Rio de
Janeiro, shore batteries opened fire but did not damage it.

Lott claimed that the president of the Supreme Court and
the president of the Congress had declared their support for the
"preventive coup." Lott also said that his actions were backed
by all the officers of the garrison in the capital, by most of the

commanders of the central and northern military zones, by the 5th Infantry Division and by the governor of Minas Gerais.

The navy and air ministers at first said in a statement that they considered Lott's action "illegal and subversive," but when the dimensions of support for the *coup d'etat* became clear, they withdrew their opposition. The coup was carried off without fighting, and Congress voted 185-72 Nov. 11 to elect Nereu Ramos, 66, as the new acting president of Brazil.

Lott was returned to his former post of war minister by Acting Pres. Ramos. These other new cabinet members were named: Jose C. de Macedo Soares, foreign affairs; Francisco de Menezes Pimentel, justice; Nelson Omegna, labor; Eduardo Catalao, agriculture; Lucas Lopes, transport; Mario Pinotti, public health; Abiguar Renault, education; Rear Adm. Antonio Camara Jr., navy; Brig. Vasco Alves Secco, air; Mario Camara, finance.

Ex-Acting Pres. Carlos Coimbra da Luz returned to Rio de Janeiro Nov. 13 aboard the *Tamandare.* He resigned as speaker of the Chamber of Deputies Nov. 14 but continued to serve as a Congressman. Carlos Lacerda went into voluntary exile in Portugal, while Col. Mamede was transferred to a small army post in the interior of the country. For a brief period, political calm returned to Brazil.

But tension developed again Nov. 21 when Cafe Filho announced that he felt his health sufficiently improved to enable him to resume the presidency. Many army officials and Congressional leaders felt that Cafe Filho might be sympathetic to elements opposing Lott's *coup d'etat* and might possibly block Kubitschek from taking office in Jan. 1956. War Min. Lott again ordered his troops into the streets of Rio de Janeiro while Congress met in special session. The Chamber of Deputies voted 179-94 and the Senate 35-16 Nov. 22 to disqualify Cafe Filho from office. The ex-president was then placed under house arrest.

Military pressure was again exerted against Congress, and Congress Nov. 24 adopted legislation under which Brazil was placed Nov. 25 under martial law in a state of siege. Cafe Filho refused either to sign the legislation or to resign, but the measure was signed by Acting Pres. Ramos.

Rail & Dam Projects

A 425-mile railway running from Corumba, capital of the Brazilian state of Mato Grosso, to Santa Cruz de la Sierra, Bolivia, had been opened Jan. 5. Presidents Cafe Filho of Brazil and Victor Paz Estenssoro of Bolivia attended the ceremony. The railway, which took 15 years to build and which Brazil and Bolivia financed jointly, was one of 2 final links in a transcontinental rail route between the ports of Santos, Brazil and Arica, Chile. It also furnished the first rail connection between Brazil and Bolivia.

Economic life in northeastern Brazil took a giant step forward Jan. 15 when Cafe Filho opened the Paulo Affonso hydroelectric dam on the Sao Francisco River, where the states of Pernambuco, Alagoas and Bahia meet. The project had been built by the government-owned Companhia Hidroelectrica do Sao Francisco for an estimated 1.8 billion cruzeiros ($24,480,000) to supply power for an 8-state area. The project, designed also to serve cities and towns in Sergipe and Paraiba states, was to bring power to an area twice the size of France and housing 15% of Brazil's population. It harnessed a water flow with a potential of 4 million horsepower.

(Coffee exports rose in 1955 to 13,696,000 sacks. As a result of high prices, dollar income from coffee rose to an unprecedented $30,366,000.)

1956

KUBITSCHEK'S FIRST YEAR AS PRESIDENT

Juscelino Kubitschek de Oliveira was inaugurated Jan. 31 in Rio de Janeiro for a 5-year term as president of Brazil. During his first year in office, he successfully confronted his growing political opposition and initiated economic innovations as the specter of inflation emerged.

A U.S. delegation led by Vice Pres. Richard M. Nixon attended the inaugural ceremony. Kubitschek's cabinet, named Jan. 30, included these 3 military leaders who had prevented an alleged coup by his opponents in Nov. 1955: Gen. Henrique Teixeira Lott, war minister, Antonio Alves Camara, navy minister, and Vasco Alves Secco, air minister. Other ministers: Jose Carlos Macedo Soares, foreign affairs; Jose Maria Alkimin, finance; Parsifal Barroso, labor; Gen. Ernesto Dornelles, agriculture; Clovis Salgado, education; the retiring Provisional Pres. Nereu Ramos, justice; Comdr. Lucio Meira, transportation; Maurcio Medeiros, health.

During a preinauguration tour, Kubitschek had been entertained by U.S. Pres. Dwight D. Eisenhower in Key West, Fla. Jan. 5, and he had told the U.S. Senate, while he was in Washington, that Brazil stood beside the U.S. in the fight against "extremist" ideologies.

Kubitschek's Economic Program

Brazil started on a new economic course Feb. 1 when Kubitschek announced a 5-year economic development program that included electric power projects as well as the establishment of an automobile industry. He pledged a "high standard of administrative morality."

To carry out his economic program, Kubitschek created by decree Feb. 1 a new Council of Development consisting of 17 persons, including nearly all the ministers of state, the director general of Brazil's civil service, the president of the National Development Bank and the heads of the military and civilian cabinents. Among the objectives of the new organization were studies to find ways of promoting Brazil's economic development. Programs also were to be drawn up to promote private initiative.

The Kubitschek administration was able to take advantage of the projects set up in 1953 and 1954 by the joint U.S.-Brazilian, French-Brazilian and German-Brazilian government development commissions to aid the country's industrial development and attract foreign capital. Most prominent were plans by the Union Carbide & Carbon Corp. (later Union Carbide Corp.) and W. R. Grace & Co. for a plastics industry.

The Krupp Co. announced that it had decided to invest approximately $25 million in Brazil in the next 5 years. Factories would be built to manufacture diesel, steam and electric locomotives and truck and automobile parts, Krupp said.

U.S. Vice Pres. Nixon in Rio de Janeiro Feb. 3 announced a $35 million U.S. Export-Import Bank loan to Brazil for expanding the Volta Redonda steel center in Rio de Janeiro State. (The Export-Import Bank revealed a $19,625,000 loan to the Santos-Jundiai Railway to buy U.S. equipment, plus another credit of $5,375,000.) Kubitschek told newsmen Feb. 7 that, while "trade relations with Russia are probable," he would not propose Brazilian-Soviet diplomatic relations.

Abortive Revolt by Air Force Officers

On the political front, Kubitschek ended press censorship Feb. 1 by executive decree and Feb. 10 lifted (effective Feb. 15) the state-of-siege measures invoked against an alleged conspiracy to prevent his inauguration.

A vest-pocket revolt broke out against Kubitschek and War Min. Lott Feb. 11 when Air Force Maj. Haroldo Coimbra Velosa and Capt. Jose Chavez Lameirao attempted to secure a series of small landing strips in the country's interior. They acted in protest against Air Min. Vasco Alves Secco's continued support of the Kubitschek administration. The 2 rebels hoped to trigger a major army rebellion against the government.

In the western section of Para State the rebels quickly seized control of Santarem, the 3d largest town in the Amazon region, and they took control of the airports of Jacarecanga, Itaituba, Belterra and Cachimbo in the Rio Tapajos area.

From Belem, the capital of Para State, a DC-3 with Air Force Maj. Paulo Vitor and 20 soldiers aboard was sent against the rebels Feb. 16. Instead of attacking the rebels, however, Vitor and his men landed at Jacarecanga and joined the rebellion. In both Rio de Janeiro and Salvador de Bahia, air force officers and men were arrested when they refused to ferry army paratroopers against the rebels.

Government forces landed and took control of Santarem Feb. 24 and captured the rebel leader Velosa Feb. 28. The rebellion collapsed Feb. 29 when the other 2 rebelling officers fled to Bolivia. Kubitschek praised Air Min. Secco for doing his duty in suppressing the revolt and for cooperating patriotically with the army and navy in an arduous mission.

Kubitschek Mar. 1 introduced an amnesty bill granting "ample unrestricted" amnesty to all accused of revolutionary activities since Nov. 1955.

The Kubitschek administration soon afterward met a much slighter sign of political disloyalty on a naval general officer's part with a determined show of strength. It ordered Adm. Carlos Penna Boto to be detained Mar. 10 for 10 days for giving an interview to the newspaper *Tribuna da Imprensa* of Rio de Janeiro. (The paper's editor, Carlos Lacerda, was in exile in the U.S.)

Maintaining an equally hard line against what was seen as the menace of disloyalty from the left, the Chamber of Deputies May 3 voted, 96-89, against the extension to Communists of the general amnesty for anti–regime plotters.

Economic & Social Developments

Dr. Willard Libby, acting U.S. Atomic Energy Commission chairman, and Brazilian Amb.-to-U.S. Joao Carlos Muniz disclosed in Washington Apr. 19 that Brazil was the first nation to receive U.S. funds (about $350,000) to build a research atomic reactor.

The Brazilian government disclosed May 1 that it would continue its sale of thorium for use in atomic reactors to the U.S. The Brazilian National Research Council had charged that the government was selling thorium at far below its real value. But pressure from the military resulted in a Brazilian National Council decision Aug. 30 to recommend cancellation of the thorium export agreement. Kubitschek Aug. 31 suspended the export of thorium and radium to the U.S. and denounced a Brazilian-U.S. accord for joint uranium prospecting on Brazilian territory. (Nevertheless, a Brazilian-U.S. atoms-for-peace agreement remained in force.)

The inflationary spiral was already gaining momentum when Kubitschek Mar. 12 signed a law granting wage increases to government workers. These totaled $200 million a year. When prices, too, began to rise, urban unrest upset some of Kubitschek's plans.

Commuters May 11 set fire to trains and stations in Rio de Janeiro suburbs in protest against a 60% fare rise. 6 persons were wounded when police opened fire on the protesters. Tanks and armored cars patrolled the city May 31 after Kubitschek ordered army, navy, and air force units to put an end to the riots. University students aided the protesting commuters but returned to classes June 11 after a successful week-long strike against the fare increase. Fares were reduced as the protesters demanded.

Other plans of Kubitschek's fared better, however. The president had formally asked Congress Apr. 19 to transfer the capital from Rio de Janeiro to Formosa Central Plateau in Goias State, 550 miles closer to the geographic center of Brazil. Preparations for the new capital, to be patterned after Washington, D.C., had been under way for 10 years. Proposals to move the capital to central Brazil had been made as far back as 1891 and had been supported by various administrations. Actual work on the project, however, was not started until 1956 under the Kubitschek administration. Through Decree Number 40,017 of Sept. 24, 1956, initial work on the planning of the new capital, to be called Brasilia, was begun. The task of building the projected city was assigned to a government organization called NOVACAP (Cia. Urbanizadora da Nova Capital do Brasil).

Brazil continued to welcome new faces to its shores. The National Institute for Immigration & Colonization and the United Hebrew Immigrant Aid Society Sept. 4 signed an agreement permitting the immigration of 1,000 Jewish families from North Africa within the next 2 years.

The country resolved a long outstanding matter of seized alien property later in September when Kubitschek issued a decree that restored prewar German assets taken during World War II. Properties that had been liquidated or incorporated into the Brazilian economy and properties of persons condemned for crimes violating national security were excluded.

Lacerda Controversy Renewed

Political unrest resurfaced in late summer. 27,000 copies of the opposition magazine *Maquis* were seized by police Sept. 7 (Brazil's 134th Independence Day), and several editors and their wives were arrested for attempting to move copies to a warehouse. The raid followed the printing by the magazine of a photostat of the first page of *Tribuna da Imprensa's* Aug. 24 issue, which had been seized by police. The page contained a manifesto by the ex-editor Carlos Lacerda, self-exiled to Portugal, who denounced Vice Pres. Joao Goulart and charged that the Brazilian army had been infiltrated by Communists. *(Tribuna* resumed publication Aug. 27 after a 3-day shutdown over the publication of Lacerda's manifesto.)

Gen. Augusto Magessi da Cunha Pereira, chief of federal police, resigned Sept. 22 in protest against a court order that he release the 27,000 copies of *Maquis* that he had seized Sept. 7. Col. Felisberto Baptista Teixeira was appointed to replace him.

In a delayed consequence of one act in the chain of events leading to the suicide of Getulio Vargas, Alcino Joao do Nascimento, who had mistakenly shot and killed Air Force Maj. Rubens Florentino Vaz in early Aug. 1954 in an attempt on Lacerda's life, was sentenced Oct. 5 to 33 years in prison. Climeiro Euribes de Almeida, one of 5 others charged with complicity in the assassination, was convicted Oct. 9. Lacerda himself returned to Brazil Oct. 11, 1956 from voluntary exile in the U.S. and Portugal.

The last major political event of 1956 took place Nov. 11 when War Min. Lott received from Vice Pres. Goulart a gold sword honoring Lott for his action in the military *coup d'etat* of the previous year.

1957

POLITICAL STABILITY & RISING INFLATION

In Brazil, 1957 was a relatively stable year politically. By contrast, the nation's economy was buffeted by rising inflation and increased spending of the Kubitschek administration as the building of the new capital at Brasilia was pushed forward at great speed.

Pres. Kubitschek addressed his more-than-58 million countrymen Jan. 1. He asserted that political stability had returned to Brazil, that democracy there had been consolidated and that the tremendous economic growth witnessed in 1956 had startled and overwhelmed everyone.

Brazil and the U.S. Jan. 12 began discussions on the granting of permission for a U.S. satellite-tracking station to be located on the island of Fernando de Noronha, about 300 miles off the coast of equatorial Brazil. Despite opposition from nationalist civilian and military elements, an agreement for the erection of the station was signed by the 2 countries Jan. 21.

Before 1957 ended, the Soviet Union began a strong campaign to open diplomatic and commercial relations with Brazil. As part of this drive, started in early December, oil-drilling and refining equipment was offered to Petrobras, the national oil monopoly, and more than 5,000 Moskvich-style automobiles were offered to members of the Military Club. Should trade relations be initiated, the Soviets indicated, the Brazilian firm

33

of Torgbras, under the direction of the retired army Col. Tito Canto, would become the Soviet trading outlet.

Year's Political Developments

The Brazilian Congress reconvened Mar. 15, with 11 political parties represented in its 2 chambers. The 326-man Chamber of Deputies and 63-member Senate were divided in this fashion:

	Deputies	Senators
Social Democratic Party (PSD)	113	22
Brazilian Labor Party (PTB)	63	18
National Democratic Union (UDN)	74	17
Republican Party (PR)	21	1
Social Progressive Party (PSP)	31	1
Liberation Party (PL)	8	3
National Labor Party (PTN)	6	0
Brazilian Socialist Party (PSB)	3	0
Popular Representation Party (PRP)	3	0
Christian Democratic Party (PDC)	2	0
Socialist Labor Party (PST)	2	0
No party	0	1

Kubitschek opened Congress by calling for curbs on inflation while accelerating public works by "raising non-inflationary capital."

Municipal elections took place in the city of Sao Paulo Mar. 27. Ademar de Barros (PSP) defeated Francisco Prestes Maia for mayor by a vote of 420,000 to 285,000. The defeated candidate had been supported by the PTB and the Brazilian Communist Party (PCB). (PCB membership was reported to have dropped in 1957 from 50,000 to 20,000 as intellectuals and students disillusioned over events in Hungary were said to have left the party.)

The political pace picked up in April when the editor Carlos Lacerda, already elected to Congress and by then UDN majority leader, charged after reading aloud from classified Brazilian State Department telegrams that the Argentine government had exerted pressure on Brazil to save Vice Pres. Joao Goulart's name from serious scandal. The scandal would have been exposed in an AP news dispatch that linked Goulart to a fraudulent lumber deal with the former Peron administration.

The Kubitschek administration, angered by Lacerda's charges, tried unsuccessfully during May to have Congress strip Lacerda of his Congressional immunity and charge him with treason. Although a majority of Congress backed the administration, the vote was only 152 against Lacerda, 132 for him, whereas the number of votes needed by the government was 164. The majority leader of the Chamber of Deputies, Tarcilio Vieira de Melo of Bahia, admitted defeat on this issue.

The press in Rio de Janeiro, where Lacerda's editorial voice had great force, reported in May that Peronists, out of power in Argentina for close to 2 years, were spending vast sums of money in Brazil for propaganda and the purchase of guns.

Partisan politics took a new turn in July, when the UDN— a party normally friendly to the U.S.—under heavy pressure from Lacerda, switched to an ultranationalistic and anti-American line of political action. The focus of this move was an effort mounted earlier in 1957 to end the monopoly in Brazil's oil development by Petrobras and to open the oil industry to Brazilian private capital.

War Min. Henrique Teixeira Lott, speaking in August at Volta Redonda, Brazil's national steel complex, urged the steel industry to share its "big profits" with its workers. Lott also claimed a role as mediator between labor and management in Brazil. *Visao,* a Brazilian business news weekly published in Sao Paulo, labeled Lott "the oracle of the nationalists trooping to his office seeking guidance or favors, which he freely grants." Other press comment charged that Lott was trying to become the spokesman of the nationalists and workers in an effort to strengthen his position as a presidential candidate in the 1960 elections.

In August, pro-administration forces introduced in Congress a bill to extend the electoral franchise to illiterates, who made up about 70% of Brazil's population. The draft law, however, was met with a determined stand by the UDN, which began a boycott Aug. 22 of all bills before the Chamber, including the proposed 1958-9 national budget.

Political tension continued into September as the UDN opposed the PSD, PTB and PSP over the new voting rights legislation. Congress finally approved a compromise registration procedure that would have all voters renew their voting certificates before electoral officials. Every prospective voter would be required to write not merely his name but also his occupation and address. Some electoral officials had been quoted as saying that 70% of Brazil's potential voters would be unable to perform this task.

Daniel de Carvalho, ex-deputy from Minas Gerais, suggested that the way to induce millions to learn to read and write was to make literacy a prerequisite to gaining admission to soccer games and to participating in carnivals. War Min. Lott continued to play a political role by coming out publicly in favor of the vote for illiterates and declaring his faith in the masses.

Local political unrest, meanwhile, seething in the tiny northeast state of Alagoas for 7 months, erupted dramatically in Maceio, the capital. Gov. Muniz Falcao of the Social Progressive Party (PSP) had been accused Feb. 14 of ordering the murder of at least 4 opposition National Democratic Union (UDN) politicians since he took office. Power and water were reported to have been cut off in the capital Sept. 13 after gunfire erupted in the state legislature between members of the 2 feuding political clans. Deputy Humberto Mendes, father-in-law of Gov. Falcao, was killed and a half-dozen other state legislative deputies wounded. 1,200 federal troops entered Maceio Sept. 18 as the state legislature voted to impeach the governor (this was the first time in Brazilian history that a governor was so arraigned), and Vice Gov. Sizenando Nabuco, a Brazilian Labor Party (PTB) member, was sworn in as acting governor. Gen. Armando Morais Ancora of the army was named federal interventor of the state.

The Brazilian press reported in September that Luis Carlos Prestes appeared to have won his year-long struggle to maintain control over the PCB (Brazilian Communist Party). A split in the PCB had been reported that June. The editor of the Communist newspaper *Democrata* of Fortaleza in the state of Ceara was ousted by Prestes after the newspaper had criticized such Communist leaders as Agildo Barata. Prestes and such other oldline Communists as Mauricio Grabois and Joao Amazones were also reported to have been under fire from dissidents. Prestes, in hiding for 10 years, returned to Rio de Janeiro in October.

During September, ultranationalists and anti-U.S. politicians reacted angrily to Brazilian press reports that the U.S. had applied pressure on Bolivia to prevent and block Brazilian-Bolivian negotiations over the 8.6 million-acre oil concession granted Brazil by Bolivia in 1938. The concession permitted Brazilian private capital to explore and exploit Bolivian oil. Brazilians would not permit private U.S. companies to do the same in Brazil.

The Brazilian press in November reported the existence of a tough colonels' clique that took the name Movimento Militar Constitucionalista (MMC), or Constitutional Military Movement, and was said to be both anti-Goulart and anti-Lott. War Min. Henrique Lott did not take part Nov. 11 in the 2d anniversary celebrations of the "anticoup."

The Kubitschek administration, reviewing its legislative record for 1957, said Congress had passed 74 of 83 bills that the administration considered important.

Year's Economic Developments

Pres. Kubitschek, in a nationwide radio address Dec. 31, gave an optimistic summary of Brazil's economic progress in 1957. Among other things, he reported that electric power had increased (by 550,000 kilowatts). Petrobras was supplying more than 40,000 barrels of oil a day, or nearly double the 1955 figure, he said—yet the nation's industries were consuming 315,000 barrels daily.

Congressman Adolfo Gentile of Ceara late in March had publicly proposed revamping Petrobras and ending its monopoly of oil development because, he claimed, the company produced too little for the sizeable amount of money it spent. His suggestion that Brazilian private capital be allowed to seek oil in 49% of the country's sedimentary areas, leaving 51% to Petrobras, evoked a sharp reaction from nationalist elements. According to Gentile, several Brazilian capitalists were eager to help speed oil production by putting some of it into private hands. Gentile named 5 so minded as Walter Moreira Salles, Teodore Quartim Barbosa, Celso Rocha Miranda, Antonio Sanchez Larragoiti and Lucas Lopez.

Kubitschek sent Congress the 1958-9 national budget in May. He estimated expenditures at 170 billion cruzeiros (more than $2 billion). Congress set about a detailed discussion of the budget in June. Members noted that there would be a deficit of 9.651 billion cruzeiros and that the military, naval and air ministries had requested 34.9 billion cruzeiros, an increase of 4 billion cruzeiros over the previous year's request.

Brazil's international economic position continued to weaken in June, and the U.S. Export-Import Bank announced a postponement of loans until Brazil cleaned house financially. Brazil's total indebtedness to the U.S. bank exceeded $600 million. J. Burke Knapp, vice president of the World Bank, said Brazil had received no loans in the year ended June 30 because Brazil was a "poor risk."

The SUMOC (Superintendency of Money & Credit), a Brazilian federal government agency, revealed June 30 that the national debt had risen to $2.272 billion. This represented an increase of more than $184.9 million from Jan. 1 figures. The largest single item, $1.463 million, was for financing special projects and for obligations of the Bank of Brazil. July figures from SUMOC indicated that dollar reserves had declined to $414 million, compared with $612 million in July 1956.

Coffee exports, which accounted for 76% of Brazil's foreign exchange and 94.8% of Brazil's exports to the U.S., had been averaging 1½ million bags a month but fell to 900,000 bags in July. Brazil's over-all trade deficit in the first half of 1957 came to $86 million.

Economic pressures on the Kubitschek administration reached what appeared to be a crucial stage in September when the government reported that it was forced to print 2.6 billion new cruzeiros. (Most of this demand for currency was created by the continuous outlay of money for the costs of building Brasilia, the new national capital.) The report also said that Brazil's dollar reserves had dwindled from $100 million to $24 million and that gold reserves also stood at $24 million.

The free-market rate in cruzeiros was listed about the same time at 80-83 to the dollar. This amounted to a 10-fold inflation as compared with the official exchange rate earlier in 1957.

Labor unrest mounted during 1957. The country's workers, suffering from the inflation, had already begun to assert themselves. Brazilians' per capita annual income had recently been reported to be $165, compared with the U.S. resident's $2,020. As inflation continued, Brazilian textile workers demanded a 35% wage increase and gave the industry until Sept. 6 to answer their demands. While a threatened strike by sugar workers was called off, bank employes demanded a 30% wage increase. 350,000 workers in the textile, metallurgical, printing and pulp-and-paper products industries went on strike Oct. 14 in a demand for a 45% wage increase. More than 11,000 state police and militia began patrolling industrial areas Oct. 17 to maintain order. The strike was settled Oct. 24 for a 25% wage increase. UDN Deputy Herbert Levy, a Sao Paulo banker, charged that textile and other manufacturers were partly to blame for the strike; he said that the manufacturers were overstocked and therefore not interested in a quick settlement.

Affected by the wage spiral, the weakened cruzeiro slipped to 87 to the dollar in October and to 96 to the dollar by December. A survey of Brazil's economy in 1957 disclosed a budget deficit as of midnight Dec. 31 of 30 billion cruzeiros; a drop in uncommitted dollar reserves to $20 million, a record low; and more than 100 billion cruzeiros added to the circulation.

The Brazilian Congress in 1957 approved an issue of 30 million cruzeiros in bonds to meet federal expenses and—so it hoped—halt currency outflows in 1958.

The 1957 survey showed that 14.3 million bags of coffee worth a total of $839 million were exported during 1957. (1956 coffee exports had been valued at $1.029 billion.) Coffee accounted for 70% of the foreign credits Brazil earned in 1957. Brazil used $250 million for the purchase of oil imports during 1957. The cost of living went up 13% during the year.

A record entry of foreign capital into Brazil was noted. U.S. investments rose to more than $1.2 billion, with more than 80% of this amount put into building and equipping factories. Mineral exports set a record in 1957. Iron ore led with 4.3 million tons, worth more than $100 million, exported; this figure compared with the 3.3 million tons, valued at $55 million, exported in 1956. Manganese exports during 1957 totaled 810,000 tons and were valued at $47 million.

Among the country's new economic moves in 1957 was the creation of a National Railroad System, which received a loan of $100 million from the U.S. Export-Import Bank.

1958

ECONOMIC ACCELERATION

In Brazil 1958 was a year of accelerated economic activity accompanied by political stability. Much attention focused on the erection of the new capital at Brasilia. The drain on Brazil's economy was noticeable as the cost of living in Rio de Janeiro climbed more than 10% between January and August. The total rise for the year was 17.3%.

Congressional, state and municipal elections held in October brought few important changes. The major political parties maintained their relative strength in the national Congress. In the southernmost state of Rio Grande do Sul, the gubernatorial victory of Leonel Brizola, brother-in-law of Vice Pres. Joao Goulart, indicated the growing strength of the Brazilian Labor Party (PTB). In Sao Paulo, the defeat of ex-Gov. Ademar de Barros for another term as governor by Prof. Carvalho Pinto indicated that the National Democratic Union (UDN) was gaining support.

Pres. Kubitschek's proposal of a general program for Latin American development, made in June, represented one of the most important thrusts in foreign policy and international diplomacy by a chief executive in the 135 years of independent Brazil's history. For most Brazilians, however, the big event of the year probably was the Brazilian victory in the world soccer games. The Brazilian team defeated the Swedish team and, for the first time, took possession of the World Cup.

Economic Events

The rapid pace of Brazil's industrialization and economic development was early in evidence. The International Bank for Reconstruction & Development (World Bank) Jan. 22 announced a loan of $13 million to the Usinas Eletricas do Paranapanema S.A. in Sao Paulo State for the erection of a power plant capable of supplying 85,000 kilowatts of electricity to south-central Brazil. The loan, the 10th from the World Bank to Brazil, raised the total of outstanding World Bank credits to Brazil to $182½ million.

The University of Sao Paulo Jan. 25 put into operation the first atomic reactor in Latin America. The reactor, a "swimming pool" type capable of a 5 million-watt output, was designed to produce isotopes for medical and industrial purposes.

Brazil's currency continued to weaken. In an effort to bolster the falling cruzeiro, banks were ordered Feb. 14 to end dollar speculation. The cruzeiro was valued at 110 to the dollar Mar. 11 as against 65 to the dollar 8 months previously.

News of further difficulties for the Kubitschek administration came with reports of a severe drought in the states of Ceara, Paraiba and Rio Grande do Norte in northeastern Brazil. Kubitschek Apr. 15 signed a 600 million-cruzeiro drought-relief bill to assist 13 million people living in a stricken area of 456,000 square miles. The situation became so desperate that a 150,000-ton airlift of food was ordered Apr. 22 to prevent starvation in the area.

The U.S. International Cooperation Administration reported May 23 that Brazil had received $3,604,000 in economic assistance from the U.S. in the fiscal year ended June 30, 1956 and $4,512,000 in the fiscal year ended June 30, 1957. Aid estimates for the year ending June 30, 1958 totaled $4,700,000. These figures did not include military hardware.

A bright spot appeared among the gloomy disappointments of the coffee trade when Brazilian Foreign Min. Macedo Soares, paying a 3-day visit to Bogota, Colombia in late May, signed with Colombian Foreign Min. Carlos Sanz de Santamaria a joint declaration on coffee policy. The

"Declaracion de Bogota" (as it was called) held that both Brazil and Colombia would fully support the International Coffee Organization set up at an international conference in January in Rio de Janeiro. The 2 countries, the "Declaracion" said, had agreed on mutual assistance in coffee trade affairs, and each had bound itself internationally to maintain stable prices and to control exports in the trade.

The 2 ministers' talks also ended in agreement on such bilateral economic matters as arrangements to study the possibilities of developing the area of their common frontier—including the Amazon River basin—and to promote mutual commercial relations. The desirability of improving river transport was a point in that accord. The 2 countries also reached agreement on the exchange of air transportation services. (In the sphere of culture, the 2 sides undertook to advance the formal study of each other's history, language, literature and geography in the schools.)

In an attempt to fight the galloping inflation, the 1958 budget was cut by 10 billion cruzeiros ($77 million) July 22. The presidential budget decree was issued in the face of an expected deficit of 32 billion cruzeiros ($243 million). The budget cut was made despite the expectation that it would slow work on the new national capital, Brasilia, formally dedicated by Pres. Kubitschek June 30 and slated for occupancy by 1960.

More U.S. loans to Brazil totaling $158 million ($100 million from the Export-Import Bank, the rest from commercial banks) were announced Aug. 8, a few days after a meeting of Pres. Kubitschek with U.S. State Sec. John Foster Dulles in Rio de Janeiro.

Brazil's economic situation continued to weaken as autumn approached. Coffee Institute Pres. Paulo Guzzo resigned Sept. 2 in a policy dispute with the federal government over declining world prices and sales. He was replaced by Renato Costa Lima, ex-agriculture secretary for Sao Paulo State.

Lima, in Washington, D.C. Sept. 24 rejected an African plan to stabilize world coffee prices; the plan would have assigned to coffee-growing countries fixed quotas on their exports at current production rates. African coffee growers, in turn, opposed an El Salvadorean plan preferred by Latin American lands. Under the El Salvadorean plan, Brazil would withhold 40% of all its coffee production from the market. Colombia would withhold 15%, Mexico 10% and all other countries 5% of the first 300,000 bags of their annual coffee crop and 10% of the balance. The African group maintained that El Salvador's plan would not stop Latin American countries from increasing production without limit. 15 Latin American countries, including Brazil, Colombia, Mexico and El Salvador, formally agreed on the El Salvador plan Sept. 27. Their aim, apparently, was to stimulate production in their own lands, where 80% of the world's coffee was usually produced.

A World Bank loan of $73 million to build a power station at Furnas Rapids, on the Rio Grande River 200 miles north of the city of Sao Paulo, was disclosed Oct. 3. The hydroelectric project was described as the largest ever undertaken in Latin America.

Inflation continued to trouble the urban population. 5 persons were killed and many others wounded Oct. 30 when police in Sao Paulo opened fire on mobs rioting in protest over a 50% rise in bus and trolley fares.

Despite administration promises, the northeast continued to be Brazil's forgotten sector. Months after the airlift of food, hunger riots broke out Dec. 5-6 in the drought-stricken area. (Damage to crops there was estimated at $75 million.) Mobs demonstrated in Natal, Rio Grande do Norte and in Fortaleza, Ceara State against inflation and alleged corruption in the government. 4,000 jobless and hungry persons Dec. 3 had sacked the town of Caninde in Ceara State.

The Kubitschek administration attempted to slow down some of the more wasteful government operations as the year came to a close. Air Force Gen. Henrique Fleuiss was named director of the National Petroleum Council, replacing Col. Alexinio Bittencourt. Col. Janary Nunes, charged with wasting and mismanagement of foreign exchange as head of the state oil monopoly, Petrobras, was replaced by army Col. Idalio Sardenberg.

The Ishikawajimi Co. of Japan began work in December on building, at Rio de Janeiro, a new shipyard equipped to send medium-sized dry-cargo ships and tankers down the ways. The Japanese firm planned to invest $8.6 million and keep majority control.

Diplomatic Developments

Shortly after U.S. Vice Pres. Nixon had made a trip to Latin America that was marked by protest riots in Peru and Venezuela, Pres. Kubitschek proposed a series of meetings aimed at improving inter-American relations. In a letter written May 28 and made public June 6, Kubitschek told Pres. Dwight Eisenhower:

I would like to send your excellency in the name of the Brazilian people and in my own name an expression of solidarity and esteem necessitated by the aggressions and attacks suffered by Vice Pres. Nixon on his recent Latin American trip.

The [general] reaction of the government and public opinion after the reprehensible acts against the courageous and calm Mr. Nixon in those countries that were the scene of those lamentable events proves that the manifestations were [on] the part of a small minority.

But at the same time, Mr. President, it is impossible to hide that Pan American unity has suffered in world public opinion's eyes. There can only result from the disagreeable events that we deplore so much, however, the impression that we do not understand one another in our... [hemisphere]. The propaganda of those interested in anti-Americanism naturally now seeks to construe those supposed misunderstandings as actual incompatibility and even enmity between the free countries of the American community—which is far from being what has occurred.

Considering, Mr. President, that is is not convenient and, mainly, that it is not just that this impression should remain—as it morally weakens the democratic cause in whose defense we are pledged—my sole purpose as I write your excellency is to transmit my conviction that it is necessary to do something to restore the presence of [hemispheric] unity. I do not have a detailed plan for this objective but, rather, ideas that I will explain to your excellency at a later date should the occasion arise.

Permit me, your excellency, to assert that we should move ahead, nevertheless, since the hour has come, to revise fundamentally the political understandings of this hemisphere and proceed to an examination of what is being done for Pan American ideals, with all the implications of this [term]. The time has come for all of us to ask whether we are moving toward establishing the indestructible union of sentiments and interests called for by the grave international situation.

As a soldier who led democracy to victory, as an experienced statesman and, above all, as a man sensitive to truth, your excellency is in a position as few others [are] to evaluate the seriousness of the question that I pose with the exclusive purpose of defining and subsequently eliminating an entire series of misunderstandings that are easily capable of being removed at this moment but may grow if we fail to pay them proper attention....

The upsetting experiences of Vice Pres. Nixon should be used for a noble task, in the sense of creating something deeper and durable and to our common destiny's advantage.

...: It is advisable to correct the false impression that we do not live fraternally in the Americas and further, in this corrective operation and in order that it may be durable and perfect, we should proceed to a true examination of conscience, as it relates to the vigor of Pan Americanism, and to ascertain whether we are on the right path.

I am sure that your excellency will appreciate that this letter is being written inspired by the best and most sincere fraternal sentiments that always link my country and the U.S....

— Juscelino Kubitschek

U.S. State Secy. John Foster Dulles and Kubitschek conferred in Rio de Janeiro Aug. 4-5 on plans to organize a meeting of the 21 American presidents to discuss economic problems of Latin America. In a joint declaration signed Aug. 6 by Dulles and the new Brazilian Foreign Min. Francisco Negrao de Lima, the U.S. and Brazil agreed to recommend that foreign ministers of the American republics meet periodically within the Organization of American States (OAS) to discuss mutual problems. The declaration added: The 2 governments had (a) reaffirmed their determination to carry out all obligations under the OAS charter; (b) expressed complete agreement to seek formulation of policies designed not only to strengthen the defense of the values of Western civilization but also to give a "greater creative momentum towards the attainment of this goal"; (c) agreed that "Latin America has an important role to play among the nations of the world" and that it was "highly desirable that Latin America take an even more active part in formulating those broad international policies which guide the free world"; (d) restated their conviction "that the strengthening of the American community requires among other measures dynamic efforts to overcome the problems of underdevelopment ... inseparable from the collective security of the hemisphere"; (e) reaffirmed "that it has become necessary to fight with determination for religious and democratic principles, for the right of nations to freedom, and for respect for man's individuality and dignity ... now challenged by the greed of atheistic communism"; (f) reaffirmed their determination to "continue along the line of broader contact and consultation already successfully started among the American republics"; (g) agreed that both governments should suggest to the other American republics that their foreign ministers should meet regularly under OAS auspices, "not just to deal with problems of immediate urgency but to discuss on a regular basis any and all problems of mutual concern, bearing in mind their common responsibilities when peace and freedom are threatened"; (h) decided to continue the consultations between their 2 countries.

(A possible crisis was averted when Communist construction worker Alberto dos Santos Moura, 43, was revealed Sept. 4 to have planned the dynamite assassination of Dulles while the latter was visiting Brasilia. Arrested Aug. 6, dos Santos Moura said he had decided not to carry through his plans at the last moment when he saw Kubitschek with Dulles.)

The outlines of Kubitschek's Operation Pan America began to appear when, in identical notes to all Latin American nations and the U.S. Aug. 16, Brazil proposed the establishment of an economic development program for Latin America. The note formalized a tentative plan suggested by Dulles on his recent trip.

Pres. Giovanni Gronchi of Italy paid a formal visit to Brazil Sept. 4-14. This was the first visit of an official nature by an Italian head of state to Brazil. Its importance was underscored by the fact that Italian immigration to Brazil had been greater than that of any European country, including Portugal. It was estimated that there were more than 3 million Brazilians of Italian origin in the state of Sao Paulo. In a "Declaration of Sao Paulo," issued Sept. 10, Gronchi and Kubitschek pledged to work for new agricultural and industrial collaboration between the 2 countries based on private initiative. Military, cultural and technical cooperation agreements were also signed.

Political & Governmental Developments

Brazilian political life came to a complete halt June 29 as the nation listened to the final game of the World Soccer Cup series being played in Stockholm. The Brazilian team defeated Sweden 5-2 to win the world championship. (Brazilian police reported June 30 that 5 persons were killed in shootings linked to celebrations of the victory. Another, excited by a broadcast of the game, died of a heart attack.)

Early in July Pres. Kubitschek reorganized his cabinet. Members of the new cabinet were: Dr. Lucas Lopes, finance minister; Francisco Negrao de Lima, foreign affairs; Carlos Cirilo, justice; Dr. Mario Pinotti, public health; Dr. Romulo de Almeida, labor; Commander Lucio Meira, transport; Mario

Meneghetti, agriculture; Dr. Clovis Salgado, education; Lt. Gen. Henrique Teixeira Lott, war; Vice Adm. Antonio Alves Camara, navy; Brig. Francisco de Assis Correa Melo, air. Adm. Jorge Mattoso Maia, navy chief of staff, was named navy minister Aug. 15 to succeed Camara, who had died Aug. 14.

Elections were held Oct. 3 for the entire Chamber of Deputies (whose membership had been increased from 324 in 1954 to 326), for ⅓ of the Senate seats and for 11 state governorships. There were no dramatic or significant changes in the makeup of either house of Congress. The Congressional results:

	Deputies	Senators
Social Democratic (PSD)	115	22
National Democratic (UDN)	70	17
Brazilian Labor (PTB)	66	18
Progressive Socialist (PSP)	25	1
Republican (PR)	17	1
Liberation (PL)	3	3
National Labor (PTN)	7	0
Christian Democratic (PDC)	7	0
Popular Representation (PRP)	2	0
Brazilian Socialist (PSB)	10	0
Republican Workers' (PRT)	2	0
Social Workers' (PST)	2	0
No affiliation	0	1

Members of the Chamber of Deputies tended to shift parties rather quickly in changes of allegiance, and alliances and new groupings constantly appeared and disappeared. Basically, however, the chamber was dominated by conservative politicians regardless of party titles. In the Senate the PSD and PTB could generally be counted on to vote together. The UDN was the opposition party, but on many issues PSD conservatives joined with UDN members to block legislation.

Of the 11 state chief executive elections, the most significant were in Rio Grande do Sul and Sao Paulo States. In Rio Grande do Sul, Leonel Brizola, Vice Pres. Joao Goulart's brother-in-law and an ardent nationalist, won control of the state on the PTB ticket. In the important state of Sao Paulo, ex Gov. Ademar de Barros lost to Prof. Carlos Carvalho Pinto of the UDN, a well-known economist who promised the electorate a reform program.

Lack of unity still existed in the Brazilian armed forces. About 70 air force officers, including several generals, were arrested Nov. 5-7 for disrespect to War Min. Lott. 16 air force generals had refused to attend ceremonies in which Lott took the oath as acting air minister during the absence of Brig. Francisco de Assis Correa Melo. An open letter signed Nov. 4 by 42 other officers praised the generals for absenting themselves from the ceremony.

1959

INFLATION & ECONOMIC EXPANSION

Except for a 2-day revolt of several civilians and some ranking air force officers in December, 1959 was a peaceful year for Brazil—but not a calm one. Political maneuvering continued to intensify in advance of the 1960 presidential race. Inflation soared, and labor tension was a major result. The Kubitschek administration pressed its program of industrial expansion; but it was plagued with financial problems, and efforts were made to obtain financing from foreign sources.

Major Economic & Industrial Developments

In his annual message to the Brazilian Congress Jan. 15, Pres. Juscelino Kubitschek added to his industrial expansion proposals with a request that the federal government subscribe 1.3 billion cruzeiros toward the construction of a 1½ billion-cruzeiro steel plant to be built in the state of Santa Catarina.

Kubitschek June 27 approved increased subsidies to Brazilian coffee planters and exporters. The Brazilian Coffee Institute agreed to pay 1,950 cruzeiros a bag for the 30% of the 1959-60 crop retained for internal consumption and 200 cruzeiros a bag for the 10% retained for fertilizer. The new crop was estimated at 30 million bags. (Brazil had committed itself to withhold 40% of its crop from export under the agreement signed Sept. 27, 1958 in Washington, D.C. with 14 other Latin American countries producing coffee.)

Increases in domestic oil production enabled Kubitschek to predict, as quoted July 24 in the Brazilian press, that within 2 years Brazil would produce all the oil it needed for domestic uses. (He also asserted that Brazil would continue his "holy war for economic redemption that millions of Brazilians have awaited.") Petrobras' annual oil output increased from 17 million barrels in 1958 to 24 million in 1959. But this was still far below Kubitschek's goal of domestic self-sufficiency in oil within 2 years.

Congress Dec. 15 passed and Kubitschek signed Law No. 3692, which created the SUDENE (Superintendencia do Desenvolvimento do Nordeste). This Superintendency for the Development of the Northeast was established to promote the economic development of 10 Northeastern states. Specific SUDENE aims included an irrigation system to aid drought-stricken farmers, and the development of mining. The new organization was to be composed of a council of 22 members and an executive staff. The council was to include representatives from the 9 Northeastern states and Minas Gerais, the general staff of the armed forces, the various cabinet ministries, the Bank of Brazil, the National Development Bank and the Bank of the Northeast. The law provided, among other things, that: Imports for industrializing the Northeast, on SUDENE recommendation, would receive priority treatment and be exempt from import taxes and duties; until 1968, specified industries using raw materials from the Northeast would be eligible for a 50% reduction in income tax and surtax; new industries established before Jan. 1964 would be exempted from income tax and surtax—provided that the output of similar industries already established there did not exceed 30% of consumption.

Battle Against Inflation

The year's battle lines in the struggle to curb mounting inflation were formed early in Congress. Brazilian Labor Party Deputy Fernando Ferrari from Rio Grande do Sul introduced a bill to bar civil servants and military officers from receiving larger salaries after retirement than they did while in service. The bill failed to pass, and it was reported in mid-January to have been blocked by War Min. Henrique Teixeira Lott.

Other unreassuring developments were reported in the battle against inflation. The administration announced early in January a 30% wage increase for government employes and the military; but Pres. Kubitschek said Jan. 27 that austerity would henceforth be the theme of his administration. Kubitschek then declared Jan. 31 that he would push economic development while cutting the budget by about 35 million cruzeiros. The reductions appeared to affect the financial demands of the transport ministry and the military.

Government statistics disclosed Sept. 6 that consumer prices ("the cost of living") had risen 33.7% so far in 1959 (by the end of November the increase was 50%) and that the cost of food had gone up 41.3%. Food shortages had begun to develop in late August because of droughts, floods and hoarding by merchants opposed to price control. (Extensive flood damage had been caused Apr. 14-16 when the Rio Negro inundated a large area in Rio Grande do Sul State. Road and rail communications were knocked out, more than 200,000 tons of rice destroyed and more than 1,200 houses washed away. Social unrest grew as drought conditions in the Northeast were reported to be spurring militancy among rural citizens. Street fighting and looting reported July 19 in the town of Bom Jardim, Pernambuco were said to have involved the Ligas Campaneses [Rural Unions]. Commuter riots took place in Rio de Janeiro in June over fare rises and bad service.)

Trucks and planes of the Brazilian armed forces began delivering wholesale meat to retail butchers and black beans to grocers in Rio de Janeiro and Sao Paulo Sept. 8. The Federal Supply & Prices Commission took this action after the major slaughterhouses had balked Sept. 4 at the commission's order to deliver meat to retailers at a wholesale ceiling price of 10.7¢ a pound. The slaughterhouses had complained that they had to pay at least 12.6¢ a pound for the meat they processed. The federal government had imposed meat rationing at fixed prices Aug. 25 because of shortages and had set the retail ceiling price at approximately 18¢ a pound for first-grade meat in an attempt to roll back meat prices to levels that had prevailed July 1. The commission warned Sept. 9 that it might seize meat from packing plants unless it was marketed immediately. (The biggest packers in Brazil were branches of the American firms of Wilson, Armour and Swift.) When efforts to force the meat packers to sell meat at controlled prices failed, the commission Sept. 29 ordered the armed forces to step up supplies to Rio butchers to 4 deliveries a week and imposed stricter rationing in Rio effective Oct. 6. Henceforth, the commission ordered, retail butchers would remain closed at all times other than on delivery days.

Spiraling prices had led to repeated strikes by workers whose wages had failed to keep pace with the cost of living. In most cases the strikes resulted in what were considered additionally inflationary pay raises. In Santos Feb. 12 longshoremen struck for higher wages and tied up the port. Recife dockworkers walked out Mar. 25 in a demand for a 30% raise. Ferryboat workers striking for pay increases paralyzed the movement of commuters May 1 between Niteroi and Rio de Janeiro on the opposite side of Guanabara Bay. In the ensuing confusion and rioting Niteroi police fired into the crowd, killing 6 people and wounding 100. In June 4,000 employes of the government steamship line Lloyd Brasileira went on strike for more pay.

The mounting wave of labor unrest and strikes finally goaded Kubitschek into threats, and he warned Sept. 3 that he would move against "subversive plans disguised as labor movements." Marshal Odilio Denys, commander of the First Army (located in Rio de Janeiro), had consulted with Kubitschek at an emergency cabinet meeting before the president made this statement. Col. Humberto de Melo, secretary of the National Security Council, repeated the warning of a possible Communist coup after coming from the meeting. Deputy Carlos Lacerda, other political opposition leaders and newspapers that reflected their views were quick to blame Vice Pres. Joao Goulart and his Brazilian Labor Party for most of the unrest. The attacks embarrassed the president, and Kubitschek denied publicly Sept. 4 that the government warning had been aimed at Goulart.

Labor problems continued to plague Brazil during November, despite Kubitschek's warning of Sept. 3. Strikes in Sao Paulo kept construction workers off their jobs, while in Belo Horizonte, capital of Minas Gerais State, public school teachers went on strike.

(One of the weaknesses of Brazil's fiscal administration had been exposed Sept. 16 when the country's internal revenue department reported that only 340,101 of Brazil's 62 million inhabitants had filed income tax returns for 1958.

(The cruzeiro-dollar relationship rose to 215.5 to 1 Dec. 22 but fell back to 196 Dec. 31.)

Foreign Funds Sought

The Kubitschek administration, faced with insufficient funds for its numerous projects, made various efforts—not all of them successful—to get loans from foreign and international institutions.

One of the unsuccessful efforts was started at the end of January when Finance Min. Lucas Lopes announced that he was discussing the possibility of obtaining new credits from the International Monetary Fund. IMF officials arrived in Brazil Mar. 16 to study the country's economic situation, but Kubitschek broke off negotiations with the IMF June 17. He asserted that an austerity program and fiscal policies suggested by the IMF for Brazil would foment additional social unrest. Speaking at the Military Club of Rio de Janeiro June 26, Kubitschek asserted that Brazil would develop its economy without foreign help. His speech seemed aimed at the U.S., which had refused to lend money to Brazil without IMF approval. Kubitschek was quoted as saying that "Brazil has come of age." "We are no longer poor relatives obliged to stay in the kitchen and forbidden to enter the living room," he declared. "We ask only collaboration of other nations. By making greater sacrifices we can obtain political and, principally, economic independence without the help of others."

It was announced later in June that because the IMF did not approve of the Kubitschek administration's fiscal policies, it had refused to provide a $300 million loan to cover Brazil's balance-of-payments deficit.

In a letter made public in July, Gov. Leonel da Moira Brizola of Rio Grande do Sul praised Kubitschek for ending the IMF negotiations. In the letter, Brizola demanded that pro-U.S. politicians be removed from Kubitschek's cabinet. (Brizola was the brother-in-law of Vice Pres. Joao Goulart.)

Sebastiao Paes de Almeida, who replaced Lopes as finance minister, said Aug. 13 that Brazil would increase its IMF quota from $150 million to $280 million despite a $300 million deficit in Brazil's balance of payments. Before he left Brazil for the annual meeting of the IMF board of governors in Washington, de Almeida asserted Sept. 28: "Brazil has no intention of seeking IMF aid." "We have enough reserves on deposit to our account in private banks to meet our normal obligations. There is no need to ask for loans or even for an extension of the payment periods of our obligations abroad." At the IMF meeting Sept. 29, de Almeida explained Brazil's position to the world banking community. He said:

● "More than half of ... [the 5%] decrease ... [in the value of world exports in 1958 from 1957] was the consequence of a drop in prices, and a sizable percentage of the total price drop concerned the primary products.... In 1956 and 1958, the free-on-board value of the exports from ... [the less well-to-do and underdeveloped] countries decreased by about 4%.... The primary producing countries, by insisting on the development of exports by means of monetary measures, exposed themselves to 2 serious evils: (a) real danger of disinvestment through loss of substance in the terms of trade; (b) disruption of their domestic development programs due to the ...[disproportionately] strong diversion of factors of production.... Unfortunately,... [the international] capital flow ... shows a tendency to decrease precisely in the periods when there is a sharp drop in the earnings from exports.... It would appear that one would be promoting the impoverishment of many in favor of the prosperity of a few...."

● IMF currency transactions since June 30, 1958 had evidenced a monetary retrenchment policy. "Such disproportion between the drawings and the repayments of currencies by the agency, during a period of decline in both volume and prices of a great number of products ... [involved in] the international trade, shows that the mechanism for financial assistance to the balances of payments is deficient in its operational process."

● "No less crucial" a factor in Brazil's economic struggle was "the demographic growth, which every year confronts us with the task of feeding, clothing, educating and housing an additional 1.6 million people. Considerable portions of the national income are thus absorbed without immediate productive result."

● "Another equally serious problem" was that of turning to profit "territory where there are vast empty geographical areas that require effective political domination. Such ... [economic] occupation also absorbs sizable amounts of capital and labor, an investment that cannot be postponed."

● While Brazil had "struggled to maintain ... a rate of economic growth higher than the birth rate" (Brazil had achieved a 12% "per capita" growth in national income), continued "massive investment" required of Brazilians "a heavy savings effort" and demanded "sacrifices that cannot be disregarded by either the national government or the governments of other countries that maintain economic relations with them in the international sphere."

● Average coffee prices had fallen by 34% between 1957 and 1959. Despite outside investment-and-financial aid totaling $1.479 billion, there was "a shortage in the availability of real factors of production for maintaining domestic levels of employment and at the same time guaranteeing the rate of investment for development purposes."

● Unless Brazil could improve domestic living conditions and attract and encourage a wide movement toward close Pan American cooperation, it would stagnate. Unless "the system of international financial cooperation" in the IMF improved, Brazil's economy would deteriorate, and it could not be a good Pan American influence. Brazil repeated a suggestion it had made earlier before the UN. This proposal called for "a system of cyclical compensation of the difficulties in the balance of payments resulting primarily from the instability of commodity prices on world markets."

● Until the IMF could see its way toward changing some of the stringently anti-inflationary conditions it imposed on Brazil for more loans and start helping Brazil become an industrialized country, Brazil had no alternative but to forgo further extensions of IMF credits.

In February, when then-Finance Min. Lopes had said that he planned to go to Washington to seek new financial aid, U.S. officials were said to have been reluctant to grant new aid without basic reforms in Brazil's budget management and credit policy. Continued U.S. government support for Brazilian economic development, however, had been indicated Jan. 12 with the announcement of an Export-Import Bank loan of $12½ million to the iron mining Companhia Vale de Rio Doce for the purchase of rail, port and mining equipment in the U.S.

An International Bank for Reconstruction & Development loan of $11.6 million to the Brazilian Traction, Light & Power Co., Ltd. for imported equipment was announced June 23 in Toronto. This increased total World Bank loans to the company to $120 million.

The International Finance Corp., a World Bank subsidiary set up to handle credit transactions of higher than normal risk with developing countries, made a loan of $1.2 million to the Companhia Mineiro de Cimento Portland, S.A. Dec. 15 for the construction of a new cement plant in Matosinhos, Minas Gerais.

Foreign Investment, Expropriation & Trade

There was evidence that U.S. private capital was maintaining an interest in Brazilian economic expansion. It was announced in January that the M. A. Hanna Corp. of Cleveland would join in a partnership with Byington Companhia in establishing a $200 million integrated aluminum industry to be built near bauxite deposits in Minas Gerais.

Verolme, a Dutch shipbuilding firm, began work Feb. 17 on a new shipyard on Jacuacanga Bay near Rio de Janeiro after ceremonies attended by Pres. Kubitschek and Prince Bernhard of the Netherlands. The yard, slated to employ more than 4,000 persons, was being built to accommodate keels of all types.

Gov. Leonel Brizola's Rio Grande do Sul state government, with the approval of the federal Mines & Energy Ministry, May 11 expropriated the concession and assets of the Rio Grandense Light & Power Corp. (Companhia de Energia Electrica Rio Grandense), an American & Foreign Power Co. subsidiary. These properties were transferred to the state's Electric Energy Commission. The Brizola state government had petitioned the federal government Mar. 29 for permission to expropriate the utility company. The state accused the company of years of infractions. According to reports from Rio Grande do Sul, the state had decided not to pay the $15 million dollars at which it had evaluated the properties.

In response to charges that Brazilian sovereignty had been violated, War Min. Lott ordered an inquiry (announced May 17) into the sale by a Brazilian firm, Empresa Navegacao e Comercio Jari, Ltd. of Belem, of 3½ million acres of Amazon River land to a U.S. group operating as the Pan-American Pioneers Co. (Pampico). The purchase had been disclosed in Washington May 2 by Douglas L. Hatch, attorney for the U.S. group. He said the project had received the "blessing" of the U.S. State Department and of the Brazilian government.

A bilateral trade and cultural agreement was signed by Brazil and Argentina Nov. 26 in Buenos Aires, where Foreign Min. Horacio Lafer was visiting Argentine Foreign Min. Diogenes Taboada. The 2 sides pledged to foster imports of each other's goods to correct trade imbalances—Argentine wheat and industrial goods in exchange for Brazilian coffee, fruits and lumber. Their total mutual trade then averaged $200 million annually.

Brazil's first trade agreement with the Soviet Union was signed Dec. 9 in Moscow. It was a 3-year agreement providing for exchanges of $25 million worth of goods each way in 1960, $37 million worth in 1961 and $45 million worth in 1962. Brazilian exports to the Soviet Union were to consist chiefly of coffee—$18 million worth in 1960 alone. The trade accord was the fruit of 2 years of negotiations by the Soviets. (Brazilian Foreign Min. Lafer said Dec. 11 that the conclusion of the trade agreement did not imply a restoration of diplomatic relations between the 2 countries.)

Hemisphere Relations

Pres. Eisenhower Feb. 26 nominated ex-Amb.-to-Italy Clare Boothe (Mrs. Henry Robinson) Luce, 55, to be ambassador to Brazil. After a bitter battle in the U.S. Senate, Amb. Luce resigned her appointment May 1, 3 days after the Senate had confirmed it.

John Moors Cabot, named by Eisenhower to succeed Mrs. Luce, was confirmed by the U.S. Senate May 28. Cabot, speaking Oct. 15 in Sao Paulo, warned Brazilian ultra-nationalists that further widening of the growing rift between the U.S. and Brazil could wreak great harm to both countries. Cabot's frequent speaking engagements before Brazilian student groups soon had the effect of reducing the students' hostility toward American influences—but not Brazilian politicians' growing distrust of the U.S. and the temptation for them to air their grievances in the approaching election year.

Pres. Kubitschek's reputation as a hemisphere leader had been enhanced when the U.S. State Department Mar. 10 made public a statement largely supporting Kubitschek's Operation Pan America proposals. The statement, entitled "U.S. Suggestions for Promoting Economic Development of the Americas," had been delivered to the members of the Committee of 21 in February. (The Committee of 21, made up of Latin American economists and political figures, was appointed by the Organization of American States to work on Operation Pan America proposals.)

Cuban Premier Fidel Castro arrived in Brazil May 5. Speaking on TV, he urged Latin America to institute programs of land reforms and to organize a common market. Castro said that only through economic freedom could people become politically free.

Foreign Mins. Horacio Lafer of Brazil and Diogenes Taboada of Argentina announced in Rio de Janeiro Dec. 8 that the 2 countries had arranged reciprocal visits of their military leaders to study defense problems, particularly against subversive activities and designs on either country. Frequent mutual consultation on political matters of common interest was also planned. The 2 men declared themselves in "complete agreement" on matters discussed at a Buenos Aires conference they had held in November, and they said that their countries had promised to "cooperate in the fight for peace" in the Americas.

(Dr. Roberto Arias, 41, accused of complicity in a plot to overthrow the Panamanian government by an armed invasion, had been given asylum in the Brazilian embassy in Panama Apr. 24 with 2 unidentified men. A safe-conduct for them to leave the country was requested the same day by Brazilian Amb. Jorge La Tour. It was reported later that 87 invaders, mostly Cubans, had landed Apr. 24 near Santa Isabel on the Caribbean. They surrendered without resistance May 1 to Panamanian troops in the village of Nombre de Dios. The surrender had been arranged by Fernado Lobo of Brazil, chairman of a 5-man Organization of American States investigating committee that had arrived in Panama Apr. 29. The invasion leader, Cesar Vega of Cuba, said the group had decided to surrender in response to appeals by Fidel Castro and his brother, Raul.)

Presidential Election Maneuvering

Making an early choice in the 1960 presidential race, Carlos Lacerda, National Democratic Union (majority) leader in the Chamber of Deputies and editor of *Tribuna da Imprensa* in Rio de Janeiro, announced Feb. 18 that he would support ex-Gov. Janio Quadros of Sao Paulo, who was not even a member of the UDN. In an interview in the city of Sao Paulo, Lacerda declared: "Not all the friends of Mr. Janio Quadros are friends of the UDN, but all the enemies of Janio Quadros are enemies of the UDN." Lacerda's newspapers Feb. 18 carried as a headline: "Immediate alliance with Janio Quadros." Juracy Magalhaes Pinto, chairman of the UDN, rebuked Lacerda. "It was premature to articulate at this moment the name of a person who was not a member of the party ... [as entitled to UDN support] for the presidency of the Republic," Magalhaes said.

The National Labor Party (PTN), a small, labor-oriented political grouping with 7 adherents in the Chamber of Deputies, nominated Quadros Apr. 21 as its candidate for president. Late in April, Castilho Cabral, a UDN (National Democratic Union) Congressman from Sao Paulo state, organized a grass-roots Janio Quadros Popular Movement (Movimento Popular Janio Quadros, or MPJQ), which organized public opinion and large popular demonstrations all over Brazil.

The Brazilian Labor Party (PTB), closing its national convention May 6, approved a motion calling for the nomination of Vice Pres. Joao Goulart as presidential candidate.

The Social Progressive Party (PSP) nominated Ademar de Barros in early June as its presidential candidate.

War Min. Henrique Lott, meanwhile, was said to be shopping for a presidential nomination. The Brazilian press had reported in mid-May that Lott would accept a nomination if several parties formed an alliance to support him.

The Social Democratic Party (PSD), to which Pres. Kubitschek belonged, began debating in mid-June on its choice of a presidential candidate. The PSD youth wing, led by Armando Falcao, PSD leader in the Chamber of Deputies, came out for the nomination of Lott. It seemed virtually assured at the conclusion of the PSD's June 19 meeting that Lott would win the nomination, but party leaders waited for Vice Pres. Goulart to return to Brazil from a trip abroad. They wanted to see whether an alliance between Goulart and Lott and between the Brazilian Labor Party (PTB) and PSD could be achieved.

The PSD July 16 officially selected Lott as presidential candidate, and Lott announced that he would continue Kubitschek's policy of rapid economic development and spending if elected. Lott also indicated that he wished to remain as war minister despite his presidential candidacy; Kubitschek approved his request. (It was pointed out in the press that Lott, as a professional soldier, had never registered as a PSD member.)

Support for Lott also came from the Brazilian Communist leader, Luis Carlos Prestes, who urged his followers to vote for Lott. Lott, however, disclaimed Communist support.

PTB leaders proposed a renewal of the old PSD-PTB alliance with Lott as presidential candidate and Goulart as vice-presidential nominee. The PSD accepted the proposal. Lott and Goulart made their first formal appearance together late in September as the candidates of the recreated PSD-PTB alliance when they opened their campaign headquarters in Rio de Janeiro. The PSD held its political convention Dec. 12 and officially nominated Lott. Since the PTB had not yet held its convention, the PSD left open its choice for vice president.

Janio Quadros, in Moscow in July while on a world tour, spent 45 minutes conferring with Soviet Communist Party leader Nikita S. Khrushchev. Quadros was quoted as urging "the most rapid possible" resumption of Brazilian diplomatic relations with the USSR. (Lott had publicly declared himself opposed to the resumption of relations with Russia.) As July progressed and press coverage increased, it became apparent that the 2 most important election issues would be inflation and nationalism. Quadros began to make famous a broom he displayed as a symbol of his intention to clean up "the mess in Brazil." Quadros returned to Brazil in September. He was enthusiastically received by Brazilians when his ship docked in Rio de Janeiro. Quadros left the boat the next day when it docked in Santos.

In a last-minute attempt to stop the UDN (National Democratic Union) convention from selecting Quadros, Kubitschek Oct. 23 suggested the formation of a new political coalition "National Union" to support the presidential aspirations of Juracy Magalhaes. The move failed to generate any backing within either the UDN or the PSD, and by Oct. 28

the president declared that he was once again giving his support to Lott.

The UDN, at its convention Nov. 8, nominated Quadros as its presidential candidate. Lacerda, Quadros' most influential supporter, held that, although Quadros was not a UDN member, his nomination was the only hope for the party to get a president more sympathetic than any since Cafe Filho to its political and social viewpoints. The vote for Quadros was 205 to 85. Party Chairman Juracy Magalhaes received the 2d highest vote. Quadros appeared at the convention after the vote and, in an emotional acceptance speech, declared that "the UDN banner will not fall while it is in my hands." With the UDN nomination, Quadros became the official candidate of 4 parties—the other 3 being the minority National Labor (PTN), the Christian Democratic (PDC) and Liberation (PL) parties. There was no unity among the various parties, however, over the choice of a vice-presidential candidate.

The UDN's view of a balanced ticket resulted in the selection of Leandro Maciel, an ex-governor of the tiny northeastern state of Sergipe, as the party's vice-presidential candidate. Quadros, reported displeased with the selection, was said to regard Maciel as a lackluster running mate.

Disagreements deepened between Quadros and the UDN, and Quadros Nov. 25 resigned his presidential candidacy. In a letter to UDN Chairman Magalhaes, Quadras said: "... I renounce my candidacy for the presidency of the republic. I have been unable ... to bring together under my banner the various groups and political currents that desired new directions for the country with the unity and harmony indispensable for the success of this campaign. I want to thank your excellency and the UDN for the support that I received at your memorable convention—and my thanks to the PL, PTN and the PDC who have also supported my name. At this phase, it is difficult thus to coordinate the efforts and bring together the ardent desires of men of good will who are battling in the various parties. It will be impossible, then, to govern and take into consideration the demands of the people and Brazilian necessities."

Quadros sent a similar letter to Gov. Carlos Carvalho Pinto of Sao Paulo State. The Brazilian press featured in headlines the new turn of events, and considerable confusion arose in political circles. Quadros Nov. 27 issued a statement repeating to the people of Brazil his reasons for resigning.

But Quadros returned to the presidential contest by informing Carvalho Pinto, in a letter dated Dec. 5, that he had decided to continue his campaign for the presidency. He said he had changed his mind in response to appeals from the party chairmen of the UDN, PDC, PTN and PL, who had allied themselves behind him. Quadros told Carvalho Pinto that he was keeping Gov. Maciel as his running mate and that the political coalition's program remained unchanged.

In an interview in the Porto Alegre newspaper *Correio do Povo* Dec. 31, Quadros explained his motive for returning to the presidential race: "What startled me, although I suspected this, was to see how many people wanted me to be a candidate for the presidency of the republic. You ask me why I returned. I returned when I saw that my wife wanted me to return. When I saw that my daughter wanted me to. When I saw that the parties wanted me to. When the workers all over Brazil wanted me to return. When the middle class, of which I am part, also wanted me to return. And above all when my opponents, with rare exceptions, did not want me to return."

Other Political & Government Developments

Under heavy pressure from politicians to alter his cabinet, Kubitschek shuffled portfolios July 22 and replaced Adm. Lucio Meira with Ernani do Amaral Peixoto as transport and public works minister. (Peixoto had resigned as ambassador to the U.S. Apr. 6 to resume the leadership of the Social Democratic Party, and Walter Moreira Salles became ambassador to the U.S. June 18.) Meira was named head of the National Economic Development Bank (BNDE). Armando Falcao, PSD leader in Congress, was named July 24 as the new justice minister, succeeding Nereu Ramos. Sebastio Paes de Almeida became finance minister, succeeding the ailing Lucas Lopes. Industrialist Horacio Lafer, finance minister during the last administration of Getulio Vargas, succeeded Negrao de Lima as foreign minister Aug. 1.

Another vest-pocket revolt—the first since Feb. 1956—began Dec. 3 and was crushed Dec. 4. It was led by retired Lt. Luis Mendes de Morais Neto, Lt. Col. Joao Paulo Moreira Burnier and Lt. Col. Haroldo Velosa, all of the air force. They were supported by a few hundred air force officers, among them Capt. Prospero Barata. Neto, Burnier and Velosa seized 3 C-47 transports at Rio de Janeiro's Galeao Airport while Barata commandeered a Panair Constellation flying between Rio and Belem, Para State. All 4 planes landed at Aragarcas, a small Goias State town on the Goias-Mato Grosso border. The rebels, who indicated fear of rising Communist power, issued a manifesto claiming that political confusion, corruption, misuse of public funds and the economic misery of people throughout the country justified the "uprising." But when the federal government landed paratroopers Dec. 4 near Aragarcas, the rebels quickly fled to Paraguay and Bolivia. Velosa seized another airliner and reached Argentina. There appeared to be no popular support for the revolt.

(Cacareco, a 4½-year-old female rhinoceros in the Rio de Janeiro zoo, won a landslide victory as a write-in candidate in municipal elections in Sao Paulo Oct. 7. The vote was seen as a protest against the high cost of living and the shortage of meat and beans.)

1960

YEAR OF PROMISE & PERFORMANCE

1960 was a busy, generally successful and promising year for Brazil. The Kubitschek administration inaugurated Brasilia as the country's new capital. One of Brasilia's first important foreign guests was U.S. Pres. Dwight D. Eisenhower. Pres. Juscelino Kubitschek visited Portugal in August. He succeeded in keeping order in early October when, for the first time in independent Brazil, an opposition candidate—Janio Quadros— won control of the executive branch in a presidential election. Before leaving office, Kubitschek became one of the most popular figures of modern Brazil.

In 1960 Brazil moved toward closer alignment with "3d-world" nations, and prominent Brazilians began to give signs of cordiality toward Soviet-bloc lands. Domestic labor discontent resulted in 2 brief but serious nationwide strikes, one of dockworkers, the other of transport workers. Brazil's financial standing at the year's end showed no improvement over 1959 because of continuing inflation.

Quadros Elected President

Ex-Gov. Janio da Silva Quadros of Sao Paulo State was elected president of Brazil Oct. 3 by the largest plurality in the republic's history. Quadros, 43, candidate of the minority Christian Democratic Party, had the support of 4 other parties, including the National Democratic Union (UDN), the major Brazilian opposition party.

Quadros defeated Marshal Henrique Teixeira Lott, 65, candidate of the ruling Social Democratic-Brazilian Labor alliance, who also had the support of a coalition that included Communists, extreme nationalists and right-wing groups. Mayor Ademar de Barros of the city of Sao Paulo, who ran as an independent backed by the Social Progressive Party (PSP), of which he was chairman, finished 3d. The vote for the 3 candidates: Quadros, 5,636,623 votes, 48%; Lott, 3,846,825 votes, 32%; de Barros, 2,195,709 votes, 20%.

Quadros, generally accepted as a brilliant eccentric, was born Jan. 25, 1917 in Campo Grande, Mato Grosso State, the son of a middle-class physician. He attended primary school in Curitiba, capital of Parana State. His father moved the family in 1930 to the city of Sao Paulo, and Janio entered the University of Sao Paulo's law school in 1935, working his way through by teaching geography and history in high school. He married in 1942 and Dona Eloa do Vale Quadros bore him a daughter, Dirce Maria, in 1944.

Quadros' political rise had been rapid and his career spectacular. He ran for and won a seat on the Sao Paulo City Council in 1945. He ran for the Sao Paulo State Assembly in 1948 on the Christian Democratic ticket and received 17,840 votes, more than any of the other 900 candidates running for assembly seats in the state. He campaigned in 1952 for mayor of Sao Paulo, and in Mar. 1953 he received 285,155 votes, defeating the candidate of an 8-party coalition. Quadros, a flamboyant political maverick, ran as the poor man's candidate with the slogan *"o tostao control o milhao* [the penny against the million]." Quadros was a reform-minded mayor. According to some sources he had inherited the management of a bankrupt city with more than $12 million in unpaid bills and a budget deficit of $6 million. A year later, when he resigned to enter the race for governor of the state of Sao Paulo, Quadros left a balanced municipal budget and $55 million in the city's treasury.

As candidate for governor in 1954, Quadros ran against 2 strong opponents, Ademar de Barros and Francisco Prestes Maia, a city planner, architect and engineer. The young ex-mayor fought every major party in the state and won. As governor, Quadros named Prof. Carlos Carvalho Pinto as the state's new finance secretary; Carvalho Pinto bolstered the state's finances and launched an industrial development program during Quadros' term, 1954-8.

Quadros won election to the federal Congress on the National Labor (PTN) ticket in 1958 as a deputy from Parana State.

Joao Goulart, candidate of the Social Democratic and Brazilian Labor parties' alliance, was reelected vice president in the Oct. 3 balloting. He defeated Quadros' running-mate, Milton Campos of the National Democratic Union, by more than 309,000 votes. (Brazilian legislation ordained separate balloting for the vice president.) Fernando Ferrari, candidate of the Christian Democrats (PDC), finished a distant 3d. The results: Goulart, 4,547,010 votes; Campos, 4,237,719; Ferrari, 2,137,382.

Gubernatorial elections also took place in 11 states Oct. 3. The victors: Guanabara—Carlos Lacerda (UDN). Minas Gerais—Jose de Magalhaes Pinto (UDN). Parana—Ney Braga (PDC). Goias—Mauro Borges Teixeira (PSD). Rio Grande do Norte—Aluzio Alves (PSD/UDN). Mato Grosso—Fernando Correa da Costa (UDN). Santa Catarina—Celso Ramos (PSD). Alagoas—Luiz Cavalcanti (UDN). Para—Aurelio Correia do Carmo (PSD). Maranhao—Newton Belo (PSD). Paraiba—Pedro Gondim (UDN).

The UDN emerged with 8 governorships in Brazil, not counting Rio Grande do Norte (Pernambuco, Sergipe and Bahia were the others); the Brazilian Labor Party (PTB) with 5 (Amazonas, Piaui, Ceara, Rio de Janeiro and Rio Grande do Sul); and the Social Democrats (PSD) also with 5 (Espirito Santo was the other), not counting Rio Grande do Norte, where a dissident UDN candidate won office with PSD support. Minor violence had taken place Sept. 16 in the city of Rio de Janeiro, where UDN Deputy Carlos Lacerda, editor of *Tribuna da Imprensa,* was campaigning to become governor of the new state of Guanabara. (His opponent in the race was Sergio Magalhaes, candidate of the Social Democratic-Brazilian Labor parties' alliance.) Lacerda was delivering an address at the Faculdade National de Direito (the National Law School) when firecrackers were thrown to keep him from speaking. Fistfights then erupted between Lacerda's supporters and his opponents

Election Campaign

The Brazilian presidential campaign had moved into focus Jan. 9, when Quadros began a tour of Brazil's Northeast. *O Jornal,* a conservative daily in Rio de Janeiro, reported Feb. 21 that Jose Ermirio de Morais, the aluminum tycoon and self-made millionaire, was Quadros' leading fund-raiser. The report said that Morais had made more than 270 million cruzeiros available for Quadros' campaign expenses.

Responding to pressures to take a more active role as the Social Democratic Party's candidate in the presidential election, War Min. Henrique Lott resigned his cabinet post Feb. 12 and was replaced by Marshal Odilio Denys, formerly First Army commander. (Gen. Nestor Souto took over the First Army. On taking command, both Denys and Souto, in their acceptance speeches, denounced "false nationalism.")

The Brazilian Labor Party (PTB) held its national convention Feb. 17 and 18. The party designated Lott as its candidate for the presidency and Goulart as PTB choice to continue as vice president. The PTB program stressed the right of labor to go on strike, advocated more social legislation, urged agrarian reform and called for Brazilian control of profit remittances to foreign companies.

Cuba grew more important in Brazilians' minds as an influence on the presidential race as Quadros announced Mar. 9 that he had accepted an invitation to visit Cuban Premier Fidel Castro. He explained that the trip was necessary for understanding Latin American affairs. (Vasco Leitao da Cunha, Brazil's Ambassador to Cuba, had returned Feb. 19 to Brazil.) In one of the campaign's most controversial moves, Quadros visited Cuba Mar. 29-31 as Castro's guest. Quadros was accompanied to Cuba by 6 Congress members (and 14 Brazilian journalists): Sen. Afonso Arinos de Melo Franco (UDN) of Minas Gerais; Deputies Castilho Cabral (UDN) of Sao Paulo, Francisco Juliao (PSB) of Pernambuco, Paulo de Tarso (PDC) of Sao Paulo, Juracy Magalhaes Jr. (UDN) of Bahia and Murilo Costa Rego (PTB) of Pernambuco. The newsmen with him included Joao Ribeiro Dantas, Carlos Castelo Branco, Helio Fernandes and Rubem Braga. Quadros cut short his visit

Mar. 31 and returned to Brazil, reportedly because the press in Havana had misquoted some of his comments on the U.S. Back in Brazil, Quadros praised what he described as Cuban reforms.

(Kubitschek, in a foreign policy address to the country Jan. 29, had said Brazil would remain faithful to the principle of nonintervention in the affairs of other American states but felt it fitting for Western Hemisphere lands to pass judgment on the behavior of any government in the world toward any other American government and "toward foreign citizens and interests in its territory." Many observers interpreted these words as an attack on Castro and Cuba.)

Chairman Luis Carlos Prestes of the outlawed Brazilian Communist Party (PCB) issued in March a 19-page manifesto urging Brazilian Communists and the country's citizens at large to support the presidential candidacy of Marshal Lott. The Communist support for Lott nagged at many of the country's voters. Asked whether the PCB should receive legal status in Brazil, Lott Apr. 30 replied that he was opposed to the party's legalization "as long as it is subordinate to or receives orders from foreign powers." "No one can dictate rules for Brazil," Lott said. (Although outlawed, the PCB held an open meeting in the Brazilian Press Association building in Rio de Janeiro Aug. 6 and called on the Brazilian government to legalize the party.)

Lott's candidacy received a strong setback in May when it was reported that his daughter, Edna, had criticized Finance Min. Sebastiao Paes de Almeida for not granting political favors to supporters of her father. According to press accounts, this criticism was couched in ultranationalistic and demagogic terms.

The Republican Party (PR) decided May 15 to cast its support in the election to Quadros. It acted after party members in convention divided, 124 votes for Quadros to 72 for Lott. Until then, the PR had been considered a staunch supporter of Kubitschek's administration.

Lott May 27 set forth a 10-point program of administration. Speaking at a political rally in Sao Jose dos Campos, Sao Paulo State, he said his program would consist of: (1) authority and morality in government, (2) balanced wages, (3) the inviolability of Petrobras, (4) nationalization and development of Brazil's energy sources, (5) educational and social welfare improvements (6) expansion of production, (7) easier bank credit facilities for producers, (8) better and more balanced regional development with emphasis on the north and Northeast, (9) national integration under the unifying symbol of Brasilia (10) international projection of Brazil and the development of Brazil's foreign trade. (Lott, campaigning May 14 in Volta Redonda, Rio de Janeiro State, Brazil's major steel town, had declared: "I affirm again ... that Petrobras is untouchable.")

Newspapers in Rio de Janeiro had reported Feb. 19 that ex-Gov. Leandro Maciel of Sergipe, vice presidential candidate of the National Democratic Union (UDN) and accepted by Quadros as his running-mate, felt that he had been abandoned by his party and had accused the Christian Democratic Party (PDC) and Fernando Ferrari, the PDC's preferred vice-presidential candidate, of being 5th columnists inside the UDN-led 4-party alliance. Maciel resigned his candidacy Apr. 24. The UDN promptly accepted his resignation and nominated ex-Gov. Milton Campos of Minas Gerais, its candidate for the vice presidency in the 1955 elections, to replace Maciel.

Quadros repeated May 28 in Porto Alegre, capital of Rio Grande do Sul State, his promise that, if elected, he would clean up Brazil. He said that he favored continuing the work on the new federal capital, Brasilia, and also that he favored rigorous controls on the remittance of profits and dividends by foreign companies in the country. He declared that agrarian reform in the Northeast was necessary. (Pictures of Quadros' reform symbol, a new broom, coupled with the slogan *"Janio vem ai"* [Janio is coming] multiplied throughout Brazil. The face of Quadros was easy to caricature and thus attracted the political cartoonists.)

Lott, campaigning in Sao Paulo early in July, warned that Brazil would find itself in the midst of a civil war if Quadros became president.

Pres. Kubitschek had said May 13, in a speech in Sao Paulo, that as president he would do nothing to help Lott's candidacy, but Kubitschek gave a luncheon for Lott in Brasilia June 8 and said: "Our stand is taken. We are on the side of Lott, in whose hands is the necessary vigor to carry the flag of development."

Kubitschek, feeling it necessary to speak out against those who favored the notion of his remaining in office after the end of his term, had chosen May 1, Brazil's labor day, to do so. He said in this May Day speech: "... I know well those who speak of *'continuismo* [continuing in office].' I know where these voices come from. They are still the echoes of those that attempted to prevent me from taking office. I know well those elements that call themselves defenders of democratic purity and [who] sow seeds of confusion and *'golpes* [revolution]'." Kubitschek, speaking to the country over the air May 2, repeated this theme. (Justice Min. Armando Falcao had been reported Apr. 28 to have dismissed as, "pure fantasy," speculations about a movement to continue Kubitschek in office after the expiration of his term. Under the constitution of 1946, no president of Brazil could succeed himself or ever have a 2d term.) Lott, speaking July 15 to the Brazilian Press Association, denounced supporters of a *"continuista"* movement to retain Kubitschek as Brazil's chief executive.

Post-Election Actions

Pres.-elect Quadros emphasized Oct. 13 that he would not be bound by party obligations in the composition of his cabinet. He said that he would continue to support outgoing Pres. Kubitschek's Operation Pan America. It was reported in the U.S. that Quadros considered himself neither a Marxist nor a rightist and that he had a reputation of advocating reform and antiinflationary measures as solutions for financial problems. Quadros was quoted as criticizing the U.S.' "unilateral concept that only private capital has a basic role in the struggle for the Latin American future." "I am favorable to free enterprise with restrictions imposed by the nation's security and social interest," he had said during his campaign for the presidency. (As campaigning closed late in September, Quadros had been reported to be suffering "almost total exhaustion." In a strenuous race he had made more than 1,000 political speeches, had traveled more than 155,000 miles and had appeared in every major town and city in Brazil.)

Quadros sailed Oct. 29 on a visit to Great Britain and other European countries. He was the first Brazilian president-elect to break with the tradition of traveling to the U.S. before taking office. Quadros avoided talks with U.S. officials in

Brazil and declined invitations from both Pres. Dwight
Eisenhower and U.S. Pres.-elect John F. Kennedy for talks
after his election.

Vice Pres. Goulart Nov. 28 departed on an overseas trip
scheduled to include Yugoslavia, the Soviet Union, Communist
China, New Zealand and possibly the U.S. He went to the
Soviet Union in December.

New Capital

Brasilia, a completely new city in the relocated Federal
District in east central Goias State, officially became Brazil's
new capital Apr. 21, 1960—Tiradentes Day. Pres. Kubitschek
reviewed a parade of 5,000 of the 40,000 troops and more than
10,000 workers who had built the new city in 3½ years.
Kubitschek was host that evening at a capital inaugural ball for
more than 5,000 guests at his residence, the Palace of the Dawn,
a modernistic structure designed by Oscar Niemeyer.

Also attending the dedication ceremonies were the
president's cabinet, most members of both houses of the federal
Congress, the diplomatic corps and Dom Manuel Cardinal
Cerejeira, patriarch of Lisbon, representing the papacy. During
special inaugural services, Cardinal Cerejeira installed at a new
altar the icon of Nossa Senhora da Esperanca (Our Lady of
Hope), a copy of the original image carried aboard the flagship
of Pedro Alvares Cabral when he discovered Brazil in 1500.

Brasilia, located on the Central Plateau, is about 550 miles
northwest of Rio de Janeiro and lies 3,000 feet above sea level.
The geographic region is a distinct zone identified by high-
altitude, subtropical-climate vegetation. The average altitude is
3,300 feet. There are 2 heavy-rainy seasons. The region has
large forested areas and wide-stretching grassland suitable for
extensive cattle raising. Jose Bonifacio Andrade e Silva,
independent Brazil's first premier, had suggested in 1823 that
the new country's capital be transferred to Goias and given the
name of Brasilia. Andrade, however, parted ways with
Emperor Pedro the same year, and his idea went unrealized for
another 137 years.

The new city's cruciform plan—an upward curved cross-
arm or curved axis as the trunkline for circulation and site of
the residential sectors, and a straight transversal or monu-
mental axis for the administration and public facilities—was

conceived by Lucio Costa, an architecture professor at the Parsons School of Design in New York, who thought of Brasilia "not merely as an *urbs,* but as a *civitas,* possessing the attributes inherent in a capital." Costa submitted his design as "a freelancer of town planning" to a jury of Brazilian architects and found to his surprise that they preferred it to all others. The main buildings for the project were executed by Oscar Niemeyer, another Brazilian architect of international renown.

The transfer of the federal capital occasioned other changes in the country's political subdivisions. In the principal alteration, the former Federal District of greater Rio de Janeiro became the country's 21st state, Guanabara—named for the major bay northeast of the old port city. Problems accompanying the federal government's official relocation gained attention after the general election of Oct. 3. Sen. Mem de Sa of Rio Grande do Sul State rose in a nearly empty federal Senate chamber in Brasilia Oct. 26 and said that in the 6 months since the new chamber had been opened, the Senate had been able to muster a quorum on only 15 occasions. In the first 3 weeks since the election, he continued, not once had a legal minimum of the membership been on hand to vote on pending legislation.

Eisenhower's Visit

U.S. Pres. Dwight D. Eisenhower paid a 3-day visit to Brazil Feb. 23-25. Beginning a 14-day good will tour of Puerto Rico, Brazil, Argentina, Chile and Uruguay, Eisenhower flew Feb. 23 to the partly finished city of Brasilia. He was welcomed by Kubitschek.

In a joint Declaration of Brasilia, prepared previously by both nations and read by U.S. State Secy. Christian A. Herter and Brazilian Foreign Min. Horacio Lafer at a ceremony unveiling a plaque commemorating Eisenhower's visit, the 2 presidents Feb. 23 reaffirmed their advocacy of: "the democratic freedoms and the fundamental rights of man"; joint action among American states to combat underdevelopment in the 2 American continents; "full implementation of the [previously stated] principles of political and economic solidarity"; "actions helping all Americans achieve improved living standards which will fortify the belief in democracy, freedom and self-determination."

Eisenhower and Kubitschek then motored through Brasilia, were received enthusiastically by the city's current population of 70,000 construction workers, and Eisenhower laid the cornerstone for a U.S. embassy to be built in Brasilia.

Kubitschek in Brasilia Feb. 23 formally proposed a 5-point economic development program to Eisenhower. The plan, previously named Operation Pan America, called for: (1) increasing lending powers of the new Inter-American Development Bank beyond its current capital of $1 billion; (2) stabilizing export prices and markets for raw materials and commodities on which Latin American nations depended for foreign earnings; (3 & 4) creating inter-American institutes for agricultural and industrial development; (5) establishing joint inter-American teams to end widespread illiteracy and raise health standards.

Kubitschek had mentioned this program in his letter to Eisenhower of May 28, 1958 as "ideas that I will explain to your excellency at a later date should the occasion arise." The economic program and the Declaration of Brasilia together formed the expression of Kubitschek's ideas for closer Pan American cooperation. (A communique reaffirming the Declaration of Brasilia was issued by Brazilian Foreign Min. Lafer and U.S. State Secy. Herter in Washington Mar. 19 at the conclusion of a 2-day visit by Lafer.)

Eisenhower flew Feb. 24 from Brasilia to Rio de Janeiro, which recently had undergone a round-up of an estimated 1,000 pick-pockets, vagrants, drunks and "criminals in general." Kubitschek had left Brasilia the night before in order to greet Eisenhower officially in Rio. After a 5-mile motorcade through Rio, whose inhabitants greeted him with great warmth, Eisenhower addressed a joint session of the Senate and Chamber of Deputies. He said the leaders of all nations had 3 responsibilities: (1) to work for the welfare of their own people and land, (2) to have good relationships with sister republics and (3) to fulfill their nation's responsibility to the larger world. Eisenhower said that self-reliance had played a great part in Brazil's remarkable industrial and economic growth but that he was proud that U.S. "public and private agencies [had] responded to the best of their ability to requests for temporary assistance." U.S. loans and public and private investments in Brazil currently totalled $2½ billion, he said.

Eisenhower's tour of Brazil was marred Feb. 25 by the tragic collision of a U.S. Navy plane with a Brazilian airliner over Sugar Loaf Mountain in Rio de Janeiro. 61 of 64 persons aboard both planes died, among them 19 members of the U.S. Navy band who had been flown from Argentina to play for a dinner Eisenhower had planned for Kubitschek. Also killed were several members of a U.S. anti-submarine team that had helped the Argentine navy in its unsuccessful hunt for an unidentified submarine. Eisenhower attended the dinner but cancelled 2 receptions. The disaster came after Eisenhower had concluded a visit to Sao Paulo, Brazil's industrial center, where he was warmly greeted by an estimated 500,000 persons who turned out in a heavy rainfall along an 11-mile route from the airport. He promised 2,000 business and agricultural leaders at a luncheon meeting in Sao Paulo Feb. 25 that "within our financial and economic capacity, we shall continue to support Brazilian development."

(After the Brazilian Foreign Office had announced in January that Eisenhower was coming, the Brazilian Communist Party made this appeal: "The party asks all members not to engage in any hostile activities, but it calls on Brazilians to make it clear to Eisenhower that Yankee imperialism is the source of all their calamities and misfortunes.")

Economic Progress & Problems

Pres. Kubitschek broadcast his 4th annual economic report to the country Feb. 5. He claimed credit, on his administration's behalf, for having accomplished 50 years of progress in 4. This, he said, was achieved by developing an automobile industry, boosting Brazil's oil-refining capacity, expanding its hydroelectric output and carrying out extensive road building. At the same time, he apologized for his administration's failure to check inflation and for the 100% rise it occasioned in living costs since he took office. Kubitschek noted with regret the slackening pace of industrialization and foreign investment in Brazil in 1958 and 1959 and cited the shortage of skilled labor and the dearth of a sound agricultural base. He called for agrarian and educational reforms and urged special development of Brazil's less-developed areas, such as the territories of Amapa, Rondonia and Rio Branco and the states of Amazonas, Para and Mato Grosso.

Budget figures released in January had revealed that the 1959 budget deficit was 40 billion cruzeiros. Figures for the 1960 budget were also announced. They indicated income estimated at 179,493 billion cruzeiros and spending anticipated at 194,327 billion cruzeiros. More than 25% of the budget was earmarked for national defense and coffee price support.

Brazilian Amb.-to-U.S. Walter Moreira Salles, speaking Jan. 28 in New York, made a detailed and sharply worded defense of his country's economic program. Citing "statistics ... based entirely on U.S. sources," Salles noted that Brazil's share of outright grants from the U.S. came to "less than $50 million in 14 years." In the same period, however, "Brazil itself contributed $39 million to the relief and rehabilitation of distressed areas" beyond its borders, he said.

Salles, putting U.S. loans into 2 categories, said that, in the first category, Brazil from 1945 to July 1, 1959 had received $649.2 million in U.S. aid coming almost exclusively" from the sale of U.S. agricultural surpluses. Of the 2d category, Brazil from 1940 to 1959 received nearly $860 million in Export-Import Bank loans and in the same period had repaid $449 million, $113.4 million of that in interest and commissions. This, Salles added, was "the 2d largest repayment made by any country."

Salles recalled having negotiated a $300 million loan from the Export-Import Bank in 1953 to relieve Brazil's balance-of-payments difficulties with the U.S. He noted that Brazil had repaid $218 million of the principal and $43 million in interest within 6 years and wondered why "this type of financial transaction is sometimes regarded with a critical eye and finds little favor nowadays." The ambassador then made an appeal for more U.S. public funds to help develop "essential programs" such as Brazil's "governmental oil industry." He added pointedly that Brazil in any case would "continue to develop" and said that "the process is irreversible, as irreversible as the development of the whole [South American] continent.

Salles concluded by commenting on U.S.-Brazilian bilateral trade from 1949 through 1958, during which period, he noted, average U.S. exports to Brazil were greater than those to any other country but Britain and West Germany. At the same time, Brazil's exports to the U.S. ranged from a high of $911 million in 1951 to a low of $566 million in 1958—well off the pace of its imports from the U.S. He attributed the "sharp decline" in Brazil's export receipts to the fall in the prices of coffee and other primary products after the Korean War and said that the Latin American countries had entered into a one-year agreement with "most of the coffee-producing countries of Africa to keep coffee exports better related to world demand." The ambassador made another appeal for the maintenance of a high level of reciprocal trade and continuous financial cooperation aimed at achieving a balance in mutual economic relations. Brazil, he said, had an "insatiable need of capital for economic development" and expected more U.S. understanding in this regard.

At a press conference in Washington, D.C. Mar. 9, U.S. State Secy. Christian Herter, when asked whether the government had ceased insisting that Brazil reach an understanding with the International Monetary Fund (IMF) before it sought further U.S. credits, replied: "No. Actually, the problems of Brazil are of such magnitude that Brazil will have to work out with various financial agencies the best way of handling these matters. The question of whether the Brazilians would take such internal steps as the IMF requires is, of course, a matter for its own decision. It is something that it is pondering, I think even now.... [Brazil] is having real inflationary problems. And, on the other hand, its internal economy has, I think, progressed more favorably than had been anticipated a year ago."

Brazil's foreign exchange shortage was partially eased with the granting of an IMF loan of $47.7 million, to be repaid in 6 months. The IMF announced May 20 that Brazil would receive $24.7 million from the U.S. Federal Reserve Bank of New York and £3,214,285 (sterling) from the Bank of England, while the Banque de France would send 24,685,285 new French francs and West Germany 37.8 million Deutsche Mark. The terms of the loan called for Brazil to repurchase the same sum in gold or convertible currency and pay it back to the IMF a half-year after completion. (It was reported that Brazil's quota in the IMF had recently been increased from $150 million to $280 million. Earlier Brazilian withdrawals from the Fund amounted to the equivalent of $260¾ million, of which $168½ million had been repaid.)

Brazilian government and U.S. Export-Import Bank spokesmen Nov. 8 issued in Rio de Janeiro a statement of agreement on a 6-month payments moratorium after Jan. 31, 1961 for $40-$50 million Brazil owed the U.S. According to their statement, the debt payment was being delayed to ease Brazil's economic problems as the new administration came to power.

A Brazilian-Soviet barter agreement concluded May 16 provided for Soviet exports including 150,000 tons of wheat valued at $10 million in exchange for 333,000 bags of Brazilian coffee valued at nearly $17 million. The first Russian shipload of wheat under the agreement arrived in Rio de Janeiro Aug. 13.

A one-year extension of the International Coffee Agreement (the current ICA was to expire Sept. 30) was signed by Brazil and 12 other countries June 11, but 4 members of the current pact—Ecuador, Honduras, the Dominican Republic and the African French Community—failed to sign immediately. (France and Portugal joined on behalf of their African coffee-producing areas Sept. 21.) The expiring ICA limited total exports to about 34 million bags annually and signing nations' exports to 90% of their sales in the best year since 1949. The June 11 agreement continued this formula but permitted these alternatives: members producing less than 2 million bags could set their exports at the U.S. Agriculture Department's production estimate due in Mar. 1961, minus 12%; those producing more could base their exports on production estimates of Mar. 1960, minus 12%. Members still were to pay 25¢ per exported bag to a coffee promotion fund.

Brazil remained the dominant coffee producer and exporter, but Colombia was giving it serious competition, and African producers, particularly those in Portuguese Africa, were becoming major coffee exporters. Under the old ICA, Brazil's individual export quota was 17,431,000 bags. Actual exports of Brazilian coffee (number of bags and value) during the years 1956-60 were:

Year	Bags	Value
1956	16,805,000	$37,710,370
1957	14,319,000	$30,991,116
1958	12,883,000	$25,339,998
1959	17,436,000	$50,127,869
1960	16,819,000	$59,376,993

Readjustments by the International Sugar Council in the world market resulted in an increase to 678,000 tons Aug. 3 in Brazil's basic export quota. The ISC's action had been occasioned by U.S. Pres. Eisenhower's order July 6 of a cut of more than 26% in planned U.S. imports of Cuban sugar in 1960. Brazil made its first sales Aug. 5 of 91,000 tons of sugar under the changed U.S. quota. The U.S. Agriculture Department announced Dec. 22 that the U.S. was assigning Brazil an 11,474-ton share of the cancelled 824,999-ton quota of Cuban sugar originally scheduled as part of U.S. imports for the first quarter of 1961. (The U.S. also distributed new first-quarter quotas among 20 other sugar-producing countries to supply the amount to have come from Cuba.)

Prospects for continued foreign investment from private sources remained promising. The Hanna Mining Corp. of Cleveland, O. had announced plans in February to invest $50 million in railroad and seaport expansion in the Sepetiba Bay area about 30 miles west of Rio de Janeiro. The National Lead Co. of New York joined with Companhia Industrial e Comercial, a Brazilian firm, in making zinc and aluminum die castings in a new plant in Sao Paulo.

Struggle Against Inflation

Throughout 1960 much of Brazil's economic activity—both governmental and private—was colored by the struggle to control inflation. A mounting wave of strikes took place during 1960 as workers fought for wage raises to keep pace with price increases.

The Kubitschek administration in January augmented its austerity program beyond fixed-price meat rationing. Decreed Laws Nos. 47, 658 and 659 of Jan. 19 indicated future government intervention in "illegal" strikes. They also pointed to a possible wage freeze and ruled out any increase in the legal wage minimum.

Kubitschek Jan. 24 ordered all government agencies to place a total of 30 billion cruzeiros ($160 million) from their budget allocations into a special reserve of funds, to remain untouched until June.

By the end of January, the cruzeiro-dollar ratio was 192 to 1—down 4 from the 196-to-1 ratio of Dec. 31, 1959.

Brazil's federal treasury Apr. 17 issued 1.8 billion cruzeiros to meet the costs of transferring the country's capital from Rio de Janeiro to Brasilia.

Kubitschek announced Sept. 29 that rising living costs were making it necessary to raise the government-decreed minimum wage. Kubitschek Oct. 15 signed a new decree providing, effective Oct. 17, for new minimum wage levels ranging from 4,000 cruzeiros (about $21.25) a month in Piaui State in Northeastern Brazil to 9,600 cruzeiros (about $51) a month in Guanabara State (the old Federal District, where the previous minimum had been nearly $32). The new minimums, applicable to state capitals and specific communities:

State	Monthly Minimum (in cruzeiros)
Guanabara	9,600
Sao Paulo	9,440
Rio de Janeiro	9,120
Minas Gerais	8,840
Rio Grande do Sul	8,000
Para, Territory of Acre	7,680
Bahia, Espirito Santo, Pernambuco, Parana and Santa Catarina	7,200
Amazonas, Territory of Rondonia	7,040
Rio Branco and Amapa Territories	6,400
Federal District (Brasilia) and Goias	6,240
Mato Grosso	6,080
Ceara	5,920
Rio Grande do Norte	5,760
Paraiba, Alagoas, Sergipe and Maranhao	'5,440
Piaui	4,000

The conservative daily *O Jornal* of Rio de Janeiro reported Dec. 23 that the cost of living in Guanabara State had risen approximately 23% in 1960, as compared with a rise of about 52% in 1959. The index of food prices had risen by 14% in the first 11 months of 1960—but the index had risen by 70% in all of 1959.

Dockworkers in all Brazilian ports Oct. 18 began a 24-hour strike for higher pay; they won a 40% wage increase.

250,000 metalworkers struck 5,200 plants in Sao Paulo Oct. 28 in a demand for a 50% increase in pay. They returned to work within a week after settling for a 40% increase and a minimum monthly salary of 10,000 cruzeiros.

More serious labor troubles erupted in November. Approximately 500,000 transport workers—railroad employes, port workers and seamen—started a nationwide strike Nov. 8 and demanded that Congress enact new schedules establishing parity between their wages and those of the military. The government, declaring the strike Communist-inspired and illegal, ordered military intervention. Kubitschek summoned Congress into special session Nov. 10, and the strikers voted Nov. 11 to return to work. Congress Nov. 23 (a) approved a wage parity law, retroactive to July 1, and (b) allocated 9 billion cruzeiros credit to cover the cost. Congress Nov. 23 also enacted salary raises of approximately 44% for civil service employes. (Sao Paulo City streetcar workers went out on strike Nov. 15 in protest against the nonpayment of back wages. They returned to work after about 5 days and received their back pay by Nov. 23.)

Other Developments

In an effort to streamline some of the federal executive branch's functions, the Kubitschek administration created 2 new ministries July 22: the Ministry of Industry & Commerce and the Ministry of Mines & Electric Energy. The former Ministry of Labor, Industry & Commerce was to become the Ministry of Labor & Social Welfare Feb. 1, 1961 when the 2 new ministries went into operation.

The Brazilian Labor Party (PTB) had put pressure on Kubitschek in April for greater representation in his administration. The result was 2 cabinet changes. Sen. Barros de Carvalho of Pernambuco succeeded Mario Meneghetti as agriculture minister and Joao Baptista Ramos of Sao Paulo succeeded Fernando Nobrega as labor minister.

Brazilian labor unions opened their 3d National Labor Congress Aug. 11, but the congress ended ineffectually after 800 delegates walked out Aug. 13 in protest over the allegedly illegal domination of the meeting by Communists and sympathizers. The Communists were accused of trying to take

over the congress by the use of 600 credential blanks stolen
from the credentials committee. The walkout against this
power play was led by the presidents of the 3 largest labor
confederations: Deoclecanio de Hollanda Cavalcanti of the
industrial workers (CNTI), Sindulfo de Azevedo Pequeno of
the land transportation workers (CNTTT) and Angelo
Parmigiani of the commercial workers (CNTC).
Representatives of the bank workers (CNTEC) and ocean river
transportation workers (CNTMF) remained at the congress.

Kubitschek Aug. 26 signed a new social security bill
increasing benefits for more than 3.6 million Brazilian workers.
(The institutes administering the program came under the
patronage wing of the Brazilian Labor Party.)

Brazil severed diplomatic relations with the Dominican
Republic Sept. 9 and closed its embassy in Ciudad Trujillo
following dispute over the granting of political asylum in the
embassy. 17 persons, including a physician and several lawyers
and university students, had fled to the Brazilian embassy Feb.
24 and had been granted asylum after Dominican plain-
clothesmen stationed near the embassy fired on them.
Dominican government sources reported later that 2 policemen
had been gravely wounded and a pedestrian killed. The
Dominican government, which did not recognize political
asylum, agreed Mar. 19 to allow the group to leave for Brazil. 2
Dominican citizens were shot and killed and 2 others wounded
July 8 in the garden of the Brazilian embassy. Brazilian sources
said they had been shot by Dominican police while seeking
asylum. The Brazilian government protested formally July 9.

Brazil continued to improve its relations with Japan. It
was announced Nov. 14 that a new immigration and land settlement agreement had been signed by the 2 countries. The new
treaty provided for an increase over the previous agreement's
maximum of 3,000 Japanese immigrants annually. Japanese
had started entering Brazil in 1908, and by 1960 there were
approximately 225,000 of them settled there. About 35,000 had
entered since World War II alone.

A U.S.-built atomic reactor was installed Nov. 11 at the
University of Minas Gerais in Belo Horizonte, Brazil. The
reactor, made possible under a 1955 U.S.-Brazilian agreement
as part of the "atoms-for-peace" program, was to be used for
research and the production of isotopes.

1961

POLITICAL TURMOIL

The political structure of Brazil was severely battered by the fast-moving events of 1961. Brazilians' enthusiasm for their new president, Janio Quadros, who took office Jan. 31, turned to puzzled anger Aug. 25 when the president quit.

The turmoil resulting from Quadros' unprecedented resignation ended only after Vice Pres. Joao Goulart agreed to accept a sharp reduction in presidential powers as the military's price for allowing him to succeed Quadros. Goulart's compromise averted a civil war and theoretically left him as little more than a figurehead under the compromise. Congress made an attempt to govern Brazil through a parliamentary system in which decisions were made by a premier and there was ministerial responsibility. Lack of party discipline in Congress resulted in a return of power to the executive office. The new system was not a success, and the country went into a political and economic decline that continued for the rest of the year.

Brazil had begun the year by asserting a new measure of independence in foreign policy. Even before Pres. Juscelino Kubitschek left office, Brazil Jan. 19 restored to full embassy status its legations in Czechoslovakia and Poland. It resumed diplomatic ties Mar. 21 with Hungary and Rumania (interrupted since 1942), established ties with Bulgaria and Apr. 6 resumed diplomatic relations with Albania. Late in November, amid much controversy, Brazil reestablished diplomatic rela-

tions with the Soviet Union, 14 years after Pres. Eurico Gaspar Dutra had ordered them severed.

Relations with a much closer country, Cuba, occasioned much foreign and domestic criticism of the Quadros administration in 1961 and even contributed to the constitutional crisis, brought on as it was by Quadros' resignation. Cuban Premier Fidel Castro May 1 declared Cuba a Socialist country and barred elections, but Quadros resisted pressure to break off relations with Havana.

Brazil's dealings with the U.S. entered a new phase. Quadros supported Pres. John Kennedy's 10-year, $20 billion Alliance for Progress program but wanted Cuba included. The mutual cordiality of the Kubitschek-Eisenhower years cooled.

Kubitschek's Stewardship

Before leaving office, outgoing Pres. Juscelino Kubitschek Jan. 16 had given an accounting of his administration. Speaking before the National Economic Council, he reported that the fall in the international price of coffee had resulted in a decline in the value of Brazil's exports. The annual value of the goods Brazil exported had amounted to $1.542 billion in the years 1951-5 but had fallen to $1.392 billion in 1957, $1.282 billion in 1959 and $1.2 billion in 1960.

Kubitschek said he felt that Brazil's inflation was not due to the building of Brasilia but stemmed rather from the high rate of population growth, the drift of the rural population to the cities and the adoption by these new city dwellers of consumer habits associated with people more economically advanced than the newcomers. He gave as another factor the unforeseen government expenditures necessitated by the long drought in the Northeast. Kubitschek accused the federal congress of adopting ill-constructed and unbalanced budgets resulting in even greater deficits.

Kubitschek reported that the growth of Brazil's domestic gross product had averaged 7.3% a year between 1957 and 1959. He maintained that the bulk of his administration's investments had been made in strategic areas of the economy, such as energy and transport.

Unofficial observers presented this somewhat gloomier economic picture: The Quadros administration would inherit an unprecedented inflationary problem. The value of the cruzeiro at the start of Kubitschek's administration was 80 to the dollar; at the end of his term it was 230 to the dollar.

The Kubitschek administration's spending exceeded revenues in all 5 years from 1956 through 1960. To cover the deficits, the Kubitschek administration had resorted to the printing press. The net result was that currency in circulation rose from 67.5 billion cruzeiros in 1956 to 177 billion in 1960.

Quadros Takes Office

Janio da Silva Quadros, 44, returned to Brazil Jan. 20 after eye surgery in London. He was inaugurated as president of Brazil Jan. 31. On the evening of his inauguration, Quadros denounced the former (Kubitschek) administration for leaving incredibly difficult financial problems for him.

"Budget deficits in the last 10 years are frightening," Quadros said in a nationwide address from Brasilia. "They rose from 1951 to 1955 to 28.8 billion cruzeiros; from 1955 to 1960 they reached 193.6 billion cruzeiros." The new president claimed that he faced a budget deficit of more than 103 billion cruzeiros. Brazil owed more than $3.8 billion abroad—$1.435 billion contracted in the past 5 years alone. "My administration must pay at least $2 billion in debts to foreign creditors," he said.

Brazil's "moral, administrative and sociopolitical crisis," moreover, was "as grave as the economic and financial situation," Quadros charged. He listed "bureaucracy ..., scandals ..., favoritism [and] *filhotismo* [nepotism]" as characteristic and said that there was "a badly made distinction between what is sacred and what is profane in [Brazilian] public life."

In international politics, Quadros said, the era of colonialism was ending. He urged that Brazil extend its hands to the younger nations of the world, regardless of their political philosophy. He also urged broader trade relations. "We are a community without rancors or fears," he declared.

Quadros delayed the speech until several hours after the inaugural ceremonies to prevent unpleasant consequences from the tensions already aroused by word of his intentions to attack the Kubitschek administration. (It was reported that outgoing Pres. Kubitschek had been determined to reply if he felt it necessary. Instead, Kubitschek emplaned for Paris. Kubitschek returned to Brazil May 5 after more than 3 months in Europe and made ready to run for the federal Senate from Goias State. In special elections in Goias June 4, Kubitschek won the Senate seat on the Social Democratic Party ticket despite the fact that investigators commissioned by Quadros had leveled charges connecting Kubitschek, while president, with various alleged frauds.)

Congress members who had supported the Kubitschek administration and were angered by Quadros' inauguration speech went into open opposition early in February. Thus, a bloc of more than 200 hostile legislators stood ready to combat the new president.

Quadros' cabinet was sworn in Feb. 1. The variety of parties and regions represented indicated to some observers that Quadros was paying his campaign debts. The new cabinet: Afonso Arinos de Melo Franco (UDN-Guanabara), foreign affairs; Oscar Pedroso D'Horta (a Sao Paulo lawyer), justice; Clemente Mariani (UDN-Bahia), finance; Artur Bernardes Filho (PR-Minas Gerais), industry and commerce; Joao Agripino (UDN-Paraiba), mines and energy; Romero Cabral da Costa (UDN-Pernambuco), agriculture; Clovis Pestana (PSD-Rio Grande do Sul), transportation; Catete Pinheiro (PTN-Para), health; Brigido Tinoco (PSB-Rio de Janeiro), education; Francisco Carlos de Castro Neves (PTB-Sao Paulo), labor; Marshal Odilio Denys, war; Rear Adm. Silvio Heck, navy; Brig. Gabriel Grun Moss, air force.

Finance Min. Mariani said after a meeting of the new Quadros cabinet Feb. 21 that the federal government's financial deficit stood at 236 billion cruzeiros. Ministers of the various administrative departments were instructed to prepare priority plans aimed at reducing expenditures by 30%.

Quadros' Reforms & Other Developments

One of the first tasks undertaken by Quadros was an attempt to clean up the country's civil service and bring order out of the chaos of public administration.

Decree No. 50273, published Feb. 17 by *Diario Official,* Brazil's "Congressional Record," ordered all government employes to report for work at 8:30 a.m. and to remain until 11:30 a.m. They were directed to return for a 2-to-6-p.m. afternoon shift. Prior to the decree they had worked one uninterrupted shift from 11 a.m. to 5 p.m.

Shortly thereafter Quadros set up commissions to investigate irregularities and inefficiency in government bureaus and government-owned and -controlled organizations. By presidential decree Feb. 27 he dismissed all federal civil servants appointed after Sept. 1, 1960. The move threw some 10,000 government employes out of jobs, according to a conservative estimate.

Quadros then surprised the nation Aug. 8 by reinstating the previous work schedule for government employes.

The Quadros administration had opened an attack on smuggling and cracked down on such then-rampant practices as avoidance of customs and black-marketing. One of the first acts of the new administration was to dismiss all customs inspectors. (The motor vessel *Alete,* en route to a private, smuggler-built port near Angra dos Reis with a $2½ million cargo of contraband, was captured by Brazilian warships Feb. 20 off Ilha Grande Bay. The ship, owned by the Gulf Stream Shipping Co., Ltd. of Nassau, Bahamas, was carrying 18 new U.S. autos, U.S. cigarettes, whisky and TV sets. The ship's capture touched off an investigation into widespread smuggling, and several businessmen were arrested.)

One facet of Quadros' presidential style consisted in sending brief memos to various government departments. He was said to have written more than 300 in February alone, and his monthly total increased.

Quadros Mar. 3 sent to his *chef de cabinet* a memo indicating his plans for monthly meetings with the various state governors. The meetings began Mar. 24 in Florianopolis, capital of the state of Santa Catarina, where Quadros conferred with Gov. Leonel Brizola. In what appeared to be part of an effort to build up a network of regional support outside of the federal Congress, Quadros arranged with the governors to allocate federal funds for various developmental projects in the states: he allocated 2.3 billion cruzeiros to help Rio Grande do Sul develop its electric power; federal financing was provided for a hospital-building program in Santa Catarina and an electric power program in Parana. The April meeting of governors was attended by the chief executives of the states of Mato Grosso, Goias, Acre and Rondonia. Quadros met May 24 in Joao Pessoa, capital of the state of Paraiba, with Gov. Pedro Gondim of Paraiba and Gov. Cid Sampaio of Pernambuco, and he stressed his interest in the Northeast region's economic development. He then returned to Brasilia, where May 31 he signed Decree No. 50681, authorizing 6 billion cruzeiros for various projects in the Northeast; the funds originated from the sale of U.S. surplus wheat in Brazil. Quadros' June 29 meeting was held in Rio de Janeiro and attended by Govs. Carlos Carvalho Pinto of Sao Paulo, Carlos Lacerda of Guanabara and Celso Pecanha of the state of Rio de Janeiro. Federal funds were granted for various projects after each meeting. *O Globo* of Rio de Janeiro reported Aug. 1 that Quadros had granted by executive order double the monetary requests of the states of Piaui and Maranhao.

A Quadros memo Mar. 3 carried orders for an inquiry into IPASE, the social security institute serving federal government workers. Lt. Col. Raul Lopes Munhoz was directed Mar. 3 to set up an investigatory staff within 10 days and to report back to Quadros within 40 days on conditions found therein. Most of Brazil's social security institutes were staffed by members of Vice Pres. Joao Goulart's Brazilian Labor Party (PTB), and Goulart May 19, in a letter to Quadros, angrily denounced the president's broadening investigation of the social security institutes.

Together with the many directives of an important administrative or vital economic nature came some unusual decrees. Quadros May 10 signed Decree No. 50578, prohibiting horse racing during weekdays. Decree No. 50620, issued May 13, forbade cockfighting. 2 Brazilian armed forces officers were arrested Apr. 15 on charges of issuing newspaper statements criticizing government policies. Gen. Idalio Sardenberg, ex-Petrobas (state oil monopoly) president, was ordered confined to Fort Copacabana in Rio de Janeiro for 4 days after issuing a public reply to Quadros' charges that Quadros had found Petrobas almost bankrupt when he became president. Adm. Luis Clovis Oliveira was arrested for criticizing Quadros' plan to place the army, navy and air force under the jurisdiction of a proposed defense ministry. A 3d officer, Maj. Luis Felipe Augusto Borges, ex-Pres. Kubitschek's former military aide, was placed under arrest Apr. 15 for 30 days for reportedly refusing to accept a new assignment in Mato Grosso State on returning from a European trip.

Left-wing Sen. Sergio Magalhaes, an ultranationalist PTB (Brazilian Labor Party) member from Guanabara, attacked the Quadros government June 13 for allegedly promoting reactionaries to key positions in the army, navy, air force and political structure.

The Communist Party Mar. 15 had issued an 11-page mimeographed document attacking Quadros and analyzing the results of the Oct. 1960 elections. The Communists charged that Quadros was not sincere in his statements to the Brazilian people and that the International Monetary Fund was running the country.

Quadros and Argentine Pres. Arturo Frondizi met at Uruguaiana, Brazil Apr. 20-22 to discuss economic and political cooperation between their countries as well as inter-American affairs in general. At the conclusion of their talks they issued a joint document (a) calling for rapid economic development in order to maintain Latin American democracy and (b) urging resistance to "direct or indirect interference by extracontinental forces" in Western Hemisphere affairs. Quadros and Frondizi simultaneously announced the agreement of their 2 countries to "permanent consultation on all matters of common interest and coordination of their action in the continental sphere."

Quadros' Economic Program

The Quadros administration's first major economic action was to order the devaluation of the cruzeiro. The move was explained by Quadros Mar. 13 in a nationwide broadcast on the gravity of Brazil's financial situation. He stressed that his regime would be one of austerity and would drastically reduce government spending. To draw up a realistic budget, Quadros said, it would be necessary to eliminate unrealistic exchange rates.

Brazil's Superintendency of Money & Credit the same day issued Instruction No. 204, under which Brazil's currency was devalued from 100 to 200 cruzeiros to the U.S. dollar. This action, in effect, cut government subsidies for petroleum, wheat, fertilizer and other essential imports. As a result, prices shot upward, with gasoline (up 80%) and bread (up 40%) leading the list of inflated living costs. Instruction No. 204 also simplified the complicated multiple exchange rate system under which certain import items received special treatment.

The International Monetary Fund (IMF) announced Mar. 14 that it had agreed to the adoption of the new Brazilian exchange system. IMF officials said they understood that the new system was only temporary and had been introduced so that more realistic rates of exchange would be obtained for Brazil's payments and receipts.

Inflation and the high cost of living had caused continued labor unrest at the beginning of 1961. In the Northeast, 12,000 railroad workers struck Jan. 8 for higher wages. About 30,000 Sao Paulo State firemen and policemen went on strike in the city of Sao Paulo Jan. 13 in an effort to pressure the state assembly into granting them a 60% wage increase. Troops, called out Jan. 14, arrested more than 300 firemen and some state policemen, including 28 officers, who had demonstrated before the palace of Gov. Carlos Carvhalho Pinto in Sao Paulo. Quadros explained his economic policies to the Brazilian people Apr. 4 and pleaded for at least one year of belt-tightening to correct the evils of the previous administration's inflationary policy.

In fulfillment of a campaign pledge, Quadros initiated a program for improving trade relations with the Communist countries. Joao Dantas, owner of the *Diario de Noticias,* a Rio de Janeiro daily, toured Eastern Europe in April and May with a mission that negotiated with Yugoslavia and Soviet-bloc representatives on proposals for increased East European trade with Brazil. On returning to Brazil, Dantas announced May 28 that he had signed agreements for $1.665 billion worth of trade with Albania, Bulgaria, Rumania, Hungary, Poland, Czechoslovakia, East Germany and Yugoslavia. Dantas also signed cultural agreements with Hungary and Rumania during his trip. Foreign Min. Afonso Arinos de Melo Franco, in recent TV interviews, had backed an expansion of Brazilian dealings with Communist countries.

Radio Bucharest had disclosed a Rumanian credit to Brazil of $50 million for the purchase of equipment for oil fields, chemical industries, agriculture and power stations. The conclusion of 5-year Rumanian-Brazilian trade and technical assistance agreements also was reported.

The Soviet government announced May 27 that Brazil and the USSR had agreed to (a) expand trade to a total of as much as $80 million a year, (b) increase their limit on mutual exchanges of "technical credit"—such as for the import of capital goods—fom $4 million to $8 million, with the possibility of further increases beyond this ceiling, (c) exchange permanent trade missions and (d) plan a Soviet trade fair in Brazil in 1962.

The Quadros administration by the end of July apparently had finished work on a comprehensive economic plan. Its first move came July 26 in the form of an executive order, Decree No. 51058, which presented a detailed analysis of Brazil's economic and social development and set priorities for applying foreign financial aid in the sphere of public investment. The decree also provided an outline for a 5-year development plan to be introduced in 1962. The additional resources needed to carry out the proposed plan were estimated to be about 95.695 billion cruzeiros in Brazilian financing and $108.1 million in U.S. currency.

In a cover story on Quadros, the Latin American edition of the U.S. newsweekly *Time* June 30 had reported these projects as part of Quadros' economic goals:

"*Highways.* Expenditures of $1 billion over the next 5 years to raise the total network from 19,000 to 27,000 miles, and paved mileage from 4,800 to 13,200.

"*Power.* Increase installed capacity from 5 million kilowatts to more than 9 million kilowatts by 1965 and 15 million kilowatts by 1970. Cost: $2 billions, half Brazilian, half foreign.

"*Education.* Reverse the Kubitschek practice of emphasizing universities and ignoring grammar schools. Goal: to increase literacy from 48% to 70% in 5 years.

"*Health.* Eliminate the corruption that swallowed Kubitschek's health plan to iodize salt (to prevent goiter [suffered by ⅙ of Brazilians]), use preventive measures to control malaria, trachoma, yaws, filariasis.

"*Northeast reform.* Combat the spreading influence of Communist-infiltrated Peasant Leagues with intensive land reform, major development under a cabinet-rank administrator. Amount allocated to date: $160 million.

"*Industry.* Provide all government help necessary to double steel production to 6 million tons yearly by 1965, set up task forces to help develop specific industries: fertilizers, petrochemicals, tractors, machine tools, heavy equipment."

The *Time* article quoted Quadros as saying: "Industry is primarily the task of private enterprise, but government must provide the necessary conditions for growth."

Quadros Aug. 5 issued Decree No. 51152, establishing a National Planning Commission, directly subordinate to Brazil's president, which was to be responsible for preparing, supervising and carrying out long-range economic and social development plans. The Quadros administration Aug. 5 submitted to Congress a bill to offer foreign companies special tax benefits as incentives for heavier reinvestment locally of profits derived from Brazilian operations. (The measure was passed in modified form Nov. 29 after the Goulart administration took office.)

U.S. Relations & the Problem of Cuba

One of the final acts of the Kubitschek administration was the negotiation of an agreement with the U.S. on the extradition of criminals. The U.S.-Brazilian extradition treaty, aimed at "the repression of crime," was signed by U.S. Amb. John Moors Cabot and Brazilian Foreign Min. Horacio Lafer in Rio de Janeiro Jan. 13. The pact, subject to congressional approval by both countries, would not apply to persons wanted for political crimes. It would give Brazil the right to refuse extradition of persons it thought would be executed. (U.S. authorities had sought these 3 Americans who had fled to Brazil to escape charges of fraud and embezzlement: Ben-Jack Cage of Texas, Lowell M. Birrell of New York and Earl Belle of Pittsburgh.)

Brazilian-American relations were reviewed Mar. 2 by Adolf A. Berle Jr., 66, chairman of a U.S. task force on the coordination of the U.S.' policies in Latin America*, and

* Other task force members: State Department counselor Theodore C. Achilles, Asst. State Secy. Thomas C. Mann, Deputy Asst. Defense Secy. William Bundy, Harvard Business School Prof. Lincoln Gordon (serving as a consultant).

Quadros at a meeting in Brasilia. Berle was accompanied by U.S. Amb. Cabot. Cabot said after the meeting that a Cuban proposal to have other countries in the Americas mediate the U.S.-Cuban dispute was not "feasible" because the U.S. regarded the matter as one of concern to the whole Western Hemisphere and not as a problem relating only to the 2 governments. The Brazilian press indicated that some coolness had developed in the talks between Quadros and Berle.

Quadros, in a May 10 policy statement, expressed opposition "to any foreign intervention, direct or indirect," in Cuba. Quadros said a Cuban government that resulted from "a clearly manifest interference by a foreign power" would never be recognized by Brazil. He pledged that Brazil would "join in measures to preserve the integrity of the continent short of intervention in any country of the [Western] hemisphere."

The ill-fated "Bay of Pigs" invasion of Cuba Apr. 17 had given rise to much comment and speculation in Brazilian newspapers. Quadros sidestepped any question framed to elicit signs of commitment by declaring that Brazil traditionally favored "self-determination." In the Northeast, Francisco Juliao, founder and leader of the *Ligas Campaneses,* organized Apr. 17 a pro-Castro and anti-U.S. demonstration. (The "Peasant Leagues" had been gaining strength in Pernambuco State; membership estimates varied from 3,000 to 100,000.) Another pro-Castro demonstration took place in Recife Apr. 23 after the Cuban rebels' invasion had been crushed.

Gov. Carlos Lacerda of Guanabara June 7 attacked Quadros' foreign policy and asked that he change his position toward "the unspeakable Communist dictatorship" in Cuba.

Maj. Ernesto (Che) Guevara, Cuban industry and commerce minister, visited Brazil on his way home from the Inter-American Economic & Social Council's ministerial conference at Punte del Este, Uruguay. The conference, which ended in mid-August, had launched the Alliance for Progress without Cuba despite Brazil's pleas. Quadros Aug. 19 received Guevara in Brasilia and conferred on him the Cruzeiro do Sul (the Southern Cross), Brazil's highest award for foreigners. Quadros said that his presentation of the honor to Guevara on Brazil's behalf was meant to "show our appreciation to the people and government of Cuba." This gesture aroused sharp and swift criticism. The most influential of Quadros' domestic political supporters, Gov. Lacerda of Guanabara, Aug. 21 strongly denounced the president's action.

In an incident involving the controversy over Cuba, Brazilian troops June 7 had ousted striking students from the University of Recife's law school. The students had gone on strike and occupied the building in protest against the school's refusal to let Celia Guevara, mother of Maj. Guevara, make a speech on school grounds. (She later addressed the students elsewhere.) The students demanded the resignation of the law school dean, Dr. Soriano Neto, who had banned the speech. Troop reinforcements were airlifted to Recife June 8 as students ignored an appeal by Quadros to return to their classes pending discussion of their grievance. Additional reinforcements were brought to Recife June 10 by 3 naval ships and planes as students clashed with troops. The soldiers dispersed demonstrators with tear-gas bombs. The strikers set up headquarters on the grounds of the Pernambuco State Legislature in Recife. The strike eventually ended June 16. (10 students at Sao Paulo's law school, supporting the Recife strikers June 9, broke street lights and upset refuse cans. They were dispersed by police.)

U.S. Amb.-to-UN Adlai E. Stevenson had conferred with Quadros in Sao Paulo for more than 2¼ hours June 11. The main topics of discussion were economic development and communism in the Western Hemisphere.

U.S. and Brazilian officials meeting in Rio de Janeiro Apr. 14 had agreed on a plan to provide Brazil in 1961 with 1,000,000 tons of surplus U.S. wheat valued at $70 million. Brazil was to repay in local currency in 40 years. 15% of the proceeds was to finance the local currency needs of the U.S. embassy in Rio de Janeiro; the remaining 85% was to pay for Brazilian public and private development programs. The agreement was signed May 4 in Rio.

U.S. Pres. John F. Kennedy Aug. 24 formally nominated Lincoln Gordon, 48, a Harvard graduate, Rhodes Scholar and professor of international economic relations at Harvard, to succeed John M. Cabot as ambassador to Brazil. (Cabot had said in July that Brazil was "committed" to the U.S. This statement reportedly prompted Quadros to remark that Brazil would tolerate no "meddling from anybody.") Gordon's nomination had been pending since late May, and the Brazilian government had approved it Aug. 11.

The Santa Maria Incident

The traditional Brazilian friendship with Portugal, the mother country, underwent a severe strain in January and early February as Brazil's political administration was changing hands. In 2 weeks of dramatic developments, a Portuguese cruise vessel, seized in the Caribbean by an armed band of 29 men led by a Portuguese political exile, called at Recife. There the rebels gained political asylum, and Pres. Quadros ordered that the ship, surrendered to the Brazilian navy, be returned to Portugal.

The episode began Jan. 22 when Capt. Henrique Carlos Malta Galvao, 65 a leading opponent of Portuguese Premier Antonio de Oliveira Salazar though once his staunch supporter, together with 23 other exiles and 6 members of the crew, took over the 20,906-ton *Santa Maria* between Curacao and Port Everglades, Fla. Galvao and his men set course for West Africa after commandeering the vessel at gunpoint. During the takeover, one man was killed and 2 injured.

(Galvao, an army captain who had spent much of his service in Portuguese Africa, was a leader of a movement that had put Salazar into power in 1926. After serving as governor of Huila, Angola, he became senior inspector of overseas territories and a National Assembly deputy from Angola. In 1947 he headed a government mission reporting on African territorial economic conditions. Galvao's investigations converted him into one of Salazar's most bitter critics. He told the National Assembly of his findings, but publication of his report was suppressed. Galvao was arrested in 1951, sentenced to 3 years' imprisonment in 1953 for subversive activities, tried again in 1958 on 13 charges, including incitement to revolt and sentenced to 16 years' imprisonment. He escaped from a prison hospital early in 1959, found asylum in the Argentine embassy in Lisbon and reached Argentina in exile the same year.)

The ship's seizure was planned as the first step in the eventual overthrow of the Salazar regime. Riots of Africans and whites in Portugal's West African colony of Angola Feb. 4-7 apparently were linked to the ship's capture. A radio message sent by Galvao from the *Santa Maria* Jan. 24 to "all the newspapers of the free world" became the first statement of the reason for the seizure. Galvao asserted that he had taken over the ship "in the name of the Independent Junta of Liberation led by Lt. Gen. Humberto da Silva Delgado, the legally elected president of the Portuguese Republic, who has been fraudulently deprived of his rights by the Salazar administration." (Delgado had received political asylum in the Brazilian embassy in Lisbon Jan. 12, 1959. Delgado, compulsorily retired by the Portuguese air force Jan. 7, had asserted that Salazar's government had ordered his arrest. He was flown into exile in Brazil Apr. 20, 1959 after the Brazilian ambassador had received a guarantee of safe conduct for Delgado from the Portuguese government.)

The seized ship immediately became an object of pursuit by U.S., British and Portuguese naval units. The rebels, after negotiating with U.S. and British officials, surrendered the vessel to Brazilian authorities in Recife Feb. 3.

The over-all plan of seizure had been directed from Sao Paulo, Brazil by Delgado. Delgado, 54, said Jan. 27 that he had planned the *Santa Maria's* capture in Sept. 1960 and had chosen Galvao as his deputy "to prepare the liberation" of Portugal. The *Santa Maria* had sailed from Lisbon Jan. 9 for a Caribbean pleasure cruise. Galvao and 23 other exiles came aboard at La Guaira, Venezuela Jan. 21. They carried false passports and had hidden arms in their luggage. The ship carried 607 passengers, including 42 Americans, and 360 crew members. The *Santa Maria's* 3d officer, Joao Jose do Nascimenta Costa, was killed and 2 crew members wounded in a brief gun battle before the mild resistance collapsed. Galvao then forced the ship's captain, Mario Simoes Maia, to sail for St. Lucia, British West Indies, where the wounded men and 7 other crew members were put ashore Jan. 24. After a Portuguese request Jan. 23 for aid in finding and returning the *Santa Maria,* the U.S. and British navies ordered ships and planes in the Caribbean to hunt for the vessel. Portuguese warships took part in the search.

Delgado directed Galvao Jan. 27 to form aboard the ship an "Independent Junta of Liberation" whose purpose would be to rally Portuguese to prepare for "operations of liberation, occupation, administration and public order." The Brazilian newspaper *O Estado de Sao Paulo* Feb. 2 published a "Proclamation of the Portuguese National Independence

Liberation Junta" issued by Galvao. It said: The "conquest" of the *Santa Maria* "prove[d]" that Salazar was "not invulnerable"; "we are at war with the Portuguese dictatorship as we are with the Spanish [dictatorship] through our integration with DRIL [The Iberian Revolutionary Directorate of Liberation]."

The *Santa Maria* was sighted in the Atlantic Jan. 25 by a U.S. Navy P2V patrol plane, whose pilot radioed a U.S. demand that the ship put in at the U.S. naval base in Puerto Rico. Galvao rejected the demand and said he was heading for Angola. But he said he was willing to meet aboard the *Santa Maria* "with U.S. authorities or any other than Portuguese or Spanish" to discuss removing the passengers. In an exchange of radio messages: Adm. Robert Lee Dennison, U.S. Atlantic Fleet commander, told the rebels Jan. 26 that the U.S. agreed to negotiate with them; Galvao said he would not dock until his status as a "belligerent" had been recognized; Dennison assured Galvao Jan. 27 that the U.S. would take no action against the rebels if they debarked the passengers.

After receiving Dennison's Jan. 27 message, the *Santa Maria* changed course and headed toward Brazil, whose president-elect, Janio Quadros (who took office Jan. 31), said Jan. 29 that he would give the *Santa Maria*'s captors asylum (Officials of the outgoing administration of Juscelino Kubitschek had warned that they would return the ship to Portugal and intern the rebels if they entered Brazilian territory.)

Rear Adm. Allen Smith Jr., commander of the U.S.' Caribbean Sea Frontier, went aboard the *Santa Maria* in the Atlantic 30 miles off Recife Jan. 31. After conferring with the rebels, Smith said that Galvao had agreed to bring the ship into Recife but that no agreement had been made on the passengers. Brazilian authorities took over the negotiations Feb. 1-2 and achieved an agreement under which the passengers debarked Feb. 2. Galvao and his men agreed Feb. 3 to accept Brazilian asylum and to give up the vessel.

(Portugal formally asked Brazil Feb. 2 to return the *Santa Maria;* it was turned over Feb. 4 to its owner, the Colonial Navigation Co. of Lisbon.)

The Brazilian government Nov. 24 granted political asylum a 2d time to Galvao, 65. 6 followers also received asylum. The exiles, however, were ordered confined to Belo Horizonte, 210 miles from Rio de Janeiro, where they were sent Nov. 30. On this 2d occasion, Galvao and his companions had arrived in Brazil on an Air France jet airliner Nov. 21 after being expelled from Morocco Nov. 14 for hijacking a Portuguese plane bound from Casablanca to Lisbon. Brazilian authorities impounded the French plane after the crew and passengers refused to continue the scheduled flight to Uruguay, Argentina and Chile with the rebels. They refused because Galvao had threatened to cause trouble on the plane if he and his friends were denied Brazilian asylum and forced to continue the flight.

(Brazil's involvement seems to have ended at this point, but the incident had far-reaching repercussions in Africa and for Gen. Delgado. Delgado issued an appeal in Casablanca, Morocco Nov. 22 to Portuguese troops to end their fight against the Angolan rebels. Delgado urged the army and other Portuguese to "take direct action" against Salazar's "dictatorial regime" and its "brutal and savage" war in Angola. He called for "a negotiated solution to Portugal's colonial problems on the basis of self-determination." Delgado, employed in Brazil, was in Morocco ostensibly to wait for his wife, who was trying to obtain a visa to leave Portugal. Actually, however, he met with other nationalist movement leaders from Portuguese provinces, whose headquarters were in Morocco.

(Galvao, Delgado and 24 others, all of whom were living in Brazil, were convicted and sentenced *in absentia* in Lisbon Feb. 10, 1962 on charges stemming from the seizure of the *Santa Maria*. Galvao received a 22-year sentence, 20 years of which were for the slaying of the *Santa Maria*'s pilot. Delgado was sentenced to 20 years. 24 defendants received prison terms of 15 to 20 years, and 7 others were acquitted. All those convicted were ordered to pay $10,000 compensation to Costa's family.

(Delgado left Brazil Dec. 18, 1963 en route to Algiers to establish a Portuguese National Liberation Front in exile in Algeria. There was no news of Delgado's progress until the spring of 1965, when his death was reported. The Spanish Justice Ministry disclosed May 8 that it had positively identified one of 2 bludgeoned bodies found Apr. 24 near the Spanish-

Portuguese border as Delgado's. The 2d body was identified May 10 as that of Arajaryr Canto Campos Moreira, 31, a Brazilian woman who had served as Delgado's secretary. The bodies had been discovered under a pile of rocks by shepherd boys in Villaneuva del Fresno in Badajoz Province, Spain.)

Quadros' Resignation

The events leading to Janio Quadros' unexpected resignation as president were apparently well under way by Aug. 18, when Gov. Carlos Lacerda of Guanabara went to Brasilia. There, it was assumed, he threatened to resign over disagreements with Quadros about foreign policy and Quadros' refusal to grant funds that Lacerda said were needed for the development of Guanabara.

Mounting tension throughout Brazil reached crisis proportions Aug. 24, when Lacerda, in a nationwide radio-TV address on the 7th anniversary of the suicide of Getulio Vargas, accused Quadros of seeking too much power. Lacerda claimed that federal Justice Min. Oscar Pedroso D'Horta had invited Lacerda to join in a plot to suspend Congress and set Quadros up as a modified dictator.

Quadros resigned Aug. 25.

His resignation precipitated a government crisis, as most of the country's military leaders, headed by Marshal Odilio Denys, the war minister, sought to block leftist Vice Pres. Joao B. Goulart, 43, elected with Communist support, from succeeding Quadros as president. The crisis found Goulart in Paris on his way home from a visit to Communist China and the Far East as head of a Brazilian economic mission.

In resigning, Quadros first sent a short note to Congress that said: "On this date and by this communication I am leaving with the minister of justice the reasons for the act in which I hereby resign my post as president of the republic."

A 2d letter declared:

"I have been beaten by forces against me, and so I leave the government. In the last 7 months I have carried out my duty. I have done so night and day, always working harder and harder without any rancor against anyone. But, unfortunately, all my efforts were in vain to lead this nation in the direction of its true economic and political liberation, which was the only way to effective progress and social justice, which this generous people are so much entitled to.

"I wanted Brazil for Brazilians, fighting for this dream in the face of corruption, lies and cowardliness of those whose only goals are to subject the general needs of the nation to some ambitious groups and individuals from inside and also from outside [the country].

"However, I feel crushed. Terrible forces came forward to fight me and to defame me by all their means with the excuse that they were only trying to collaborate. Had I remained at my post I would share no longer the confidence and peace necessary to carry on with my duties. I believe that I would not even be able to maintain public peace.

"Here I call a halt with my thoughts turned toward the people, the students and the workers and also to the whole family of our country. Here I close this page of my life and of the nation's life. I do not lack the courage to do so.

"I leave with an appeal and expression of gratitude. I wish to proclaim at this moment my gratitude to those who have helped me inside and outside my administration and especially to the armed forces whose conduct has been exemplary in all instances.

"My appeal is that order and respect should be maintained by one and all. Only thus will we maintain our dignity in this country and in the world. Only thus will we maintain the dignity of our past and our Christian destiny.

"I return now to my work as lawyer and teacher. Let us all work. There are many ways of serving our nation."

(Quadros, his wife and daughter sailed Aug. 28 aboard the British liner *Uruguay Star* for a visit to Europe at his own expense.)

Congress accepted Quadros' resignation and named Chamber of Deputies Speaker Ranieri Mazzili as interim president.

Quadros' resignation touched off a student demonstration in Rio de Janeiro that was broken up by police using tear gas. A mob of about 500 persons stoned the U.S. embassy in Rio de Janeiro and broke several windows. Other anti-U.S. demonstrators threw tear gas grenades into the U.S. Information Service office before they were dispersed by police.

Retired Marshal Henrique Teixeira Lott, an unsuccessful presidential candidate in 1960, was arrested Aug. 27 after charging Aug. 26 that War Min. Odilio Denys was planning to prevent Joao Goulart from assuming the presidency and to arrest Goulart on his arrival from Europe. Lott was charged with making an inflamatory statement. A bank holiday was declared Aug. 28, and news censorship was imposed. Military police in Rio de Janeiro used tear gas to repel a leftist rally of 2,000 pro-Goulart supporters.

Interim Pres. Mazzili reported to Congress Aug. 28 that the military leaders opposed Goulart's succession to the presidency "for reasons of national security." Mazzili made the statement after meeting earlier Aug. 28 in Brasilia with War Min. Denys, Navy Min. Silvio Heck and Air Min. Gabriel Grun Moss. (Denys, asserting Aug. 27 that he opposed Goulart's governmental philosophy, had said the time had come to choose between "communism and Brazil.")

Goulart told newsmen in Paris Aug. 29 that he would return to Brazil to assume the presidency and "fulfill the constitutional duties that are imposed on me." But Denys, Heck and Moss declared in a manifesto Aug. 30 that they remained opposed to Goulart's return to Brazil "in the present situation." The National Security Council, a group of high military and civilian officials, refused to support their manifesto.

The commander of the 3d Army, Gen. Jose Machado Lopes, was reported Aug. 29 to have come out in support of Goulart. A 3d Army envoy reportedly informed Denys that Lopes would take orders only from Goulart. The Guaiba radio, in a broadcast from the Rio Grande do Sul city of Porto Alegre, declared Aug. 29 that the 3d Army and the 5th Air Force, whose headquarters were in Porto Alegre, would no longer take orders from the "reactionary" war minister. The broadcast announced that a joint statement had been issued by Lopes and Gov. Leonel Brizola, Goulart's brother-in-law, calling on the 2d Army in Sao Paulo and the civilians "to back the revolution."

The Goias, Santa Catarina and Parana state governors also gave their support to Goulart. The Goias governor called on the people "to fight" if need be to assure Goulart's succession to office. Pro-Goulart broadcasts were conducted by 5 large radio stations (dubbed "the liberty network") from Rio Grande do Sul State.

The Soviet news agency Tass charged Aug. 26 that Quadros' resignation had been forced by U.S. economic pressure and by U.S. displeasure with Quadros' "independent foreign policy." Tass said the U.S. had been dissatisfied with Quadros' "refusal to support [U.S.] stratagems against Cuba and" his policy "to normalize do Sul State. countries in the Socialist camp." (The Brazilian Foreign Ministry Aug. 29 suspended negotiations for the resumption of Brazilian-Soviet ties.

The text of an exchange of letters between Soviet Premier Nikita S. Khrushchev and Quadros, setting the stage for a resumption of Soviet-Brazilian diplomatic relations, had been published in Moscow by *Izvestia* Aug. 25 and *Pravda* Aug. 26.)

A U.S. State Department statement Aug. 26 denied "irresponsible charges" by "international mischief makers" that the U.S. had pressured Quadros to resign. The statement, citing U.S. agreement to provide Brazil with large-scale economic aid, said U.S.-Brazilian relations had been "friendly and close."

Cuban Premier Fidel Castro Aug. 26 attributed Quadros' resignation to a "treacherous stroke of imperialism's paw." Praising Quadros as a defender of Cuba "against [U.S.] intervention," Castro called the ex-Brazilian president "one of the staunchest supporters of self-determination." In a TV address Aug. 29, Castro advised Brazilians to wage guerrilla warfare against "reactionary militarists" who, he charged, were responsible for forcing Quadros out of office.

Constitution Amended to End Crisis

The Brazilian Congress, in a Saturday session Sept. 2, approved a constitutional amendment curbing the powers of the presidency and creating a parliamentary form of government. The purpose of the amendment was to quiet objections to Goulart's becoming president and thus to end the crisis that had started with Quadros' resignation. The amendment helped overcome Brazilian military leaders' opposition to Goulart. The Congressional action also averted a military clash between pro- and anti-Goulart forces.

The constitutional amendment, approved by the Chamber of Deputies (263 to 55) and by the Senate (48 to 6), provided that:

(a) A Congressionally elected president would appoint a premier with the approval of the Chamber of Deputies; the premier, as president of the Council of Ministers (cabinet), would exercise the executive powers formerly wielded by the president.

(b) Presidential vetoes of legislation could be overridden by a ⅔ vote of both houses of Congress.

(c) All laws signed by the president required countersignatures of the premier and the government agency head involved.

(d) The president would have power to dissolve Congress after a series of no-confidence votes but was required to call for Congressional elections within 90 days of Congress' dissolution; the old Congress would remain in office pending such elections.

(e) The president could be impeached for such crimes as (1) attempting to curb federal or state governments' institutional powers, (2) seeking to limit individual freedoms or (3) endangering internal security.

(f) A plebiscite would be held in 1965 to determine whether to continue the new parliamentary form of government or to revert to the previous system of a strong president.

Goulart, who was supposed to serve until Jan. 31, 1966 (the expiration of Quadros' term), had agreed to the constitutional amendment after meeting with a Brazilian delegation in Montevideo.

Sen. Juscelino Kubitschek, ex-president and a Goulart supporter, expressed opposition to the new law Sept. 2. Rio Grande do Sul State Gov. Leonel Brizola, also a Goulart backer, charged that the change-over to a parliamentary system was approved by Congress "under military pressure."

War Min. Denys, Navy Min. Heck and Air Min. Moss Sept. 3 formally approved the constitutional amendment and Goulart's inauguration as president.

Opposition to Goulart Quelled

Goulart arrived by plane in Brasilia Sept. 5 to take the presidential oath of office. He came from the Rio Grande do Sul State capital of Porto Alegre, a pro-Goulart stronghold, where he had arrived Sept. 1 from Paris after stop-overs in New York Aug. 30 and in Montevideo, Uruguay Aug. 31. Before Goulart reached Brasilia, the war, navy and air ministers had flown there earlier Sept. 5 to quell a group of dissident air force officers who had closed the Brasilia airport Sept. 4 and threatened to shoot down Goulart's plane.

The resolution of the crisis was preceded by a series of government military moves aimed at the pro-Goulart 3d Army, commanded by Gen. Lopes, in Rio Grande do Sul State. No actual clashes occurred despite a buildup of forces on both sides. A 3d Army communique issued by Lopes Aug. 31 had disclosed that government naval infantry had landed at the Santa Catarina State ports of Laguna and Florianopolis, about 330 miles north of Porto Alegre, 3d Army headquarters. Lopes defied a War Ministry order that he and his aides present themselves to the ministry within 8 days or be considered deserters.

A navy communique Sept. 1 announced that government warships had "taken strategic positions" off Rio Grande do Sul "to support [armed] action" "if necessary."

A Porto Alegre broadcast Sept. 1 asserted that the city would be proclaimed Brazil's new capital if Goulart were blocked from the presidency. The broadcast said the 2d and 4th Armies had joined the 3d Army as "the forces of legality" against the military leaders.

The Porto Alegre newspaper *O Globo* reported Sept. 2 that the 3d Army had stationed artillery at the entrance to Lagoa dos Patos, the bay leading to the port. 3 barges had been sunk in the bay to block the port to hostile ships.

A navy communique Sept. 3 reported that the Florianopolis troops had been withdrawn to avoid clashes with 3d Army troops in adjacent Rio Grande do Sul. A 3d Army unit approached Laguna Sept. 3 but withdrew in the face of an ultimatum from Adm. Clovis de Oliveira, commander of government forces in the area. First and 2d Army troops that had been sent to the borders of Sao Paulo and Parana states were reported Sept. 4 to be moving southward in the direction of 3d Army forces.

Goulart Becomes President

Joao Belchoir Marques (Jango) Goulart was inaugurated as president of Brazil Sept. 7 before a joint session of Congress in Brasilia.

The new president was born Mar. 1, 1918 in Sao Borja, Rio Grande do Sul. He studied law at the University of Porto Alegre, received his degree in 1939, then returned to his favorite occupation, ranching, and managed his father's estates 1939-45. When Getulio Vargas was deposed in 1945 and returned to his ranch at Sao Borja, which bordered Goulart's ranch, Goulart became a frequent visitor and warm friend of Vargas. Goulart entered the PTB (Brazilian Labor Party) in 1945 and was elected a state assemblyman on the PTB ticket in 1947. Goulart played an important role in Vargas' 1950 presidential campaign and was elected a federal Congressman. Vargas made Goulart his labor minister, and he served in 1953-4 until the army demanded his removal on suspicion of building a Peronista machine in Brazil. Goulart was elected vice president in 1955 as the running mate of Juscelino Kubitschek. Goulart was reelected vice president in 1960. Married to the former Maria Tereza Fontela, he had 2 children.

In his inaugural address, Goulart urged Brazilians to unite for "the only internal fight we should have, which is for our economic liberation." We must find a solution to the problems of the common people," he said.

Goulart appointed an 11-man coalition cabinet headed by Dr. Tancredo de Almeida Neves, 51, as premier and justice minister. (Neves was described as a conservative on financial matters and a Goulart supporter against the military.) Congress approved the cabinet Sept. 8 by 259-22 vote. The cabinet's party composition: Social Democratic Party, 6 (including Neves); National Democratic Union Party, 2; Brazilian Labor Party, 2; Christian Democratic Party, one. The cabinet included 3 new armed forces ministers; they replaced War Min. Odilio Denys, Navy Min. Silvio Heck and Air Min. Gabriel Grun Moss, who had resigned in opposition to Goulart.

Members of the cabinet: Premier and Justice—Dr. Tancredo Neves; Foreign—Francisco San Tiago Dantas; Finance—Walter Moreira Salles; War—Gen. Jose Segadas Viana; Navy—Adm. Angelio Valasco de Almeida; Air—Brig. Clovis Travasso; Agriculture—Armando Monteiro Jr.; Transportation—Virgilio Tavora; Mines & Energy—Gabrial Resende Passos; Industry & Commerce—Ulisses Guimaraes; Labor & Welfare—Andre Franco Montoro; Education— Armando Oliveira Brito; Health—Estacio Souto Maior.

Policy on Cuba & Red Nations Affirmed

A cabinet communique issued Sept. 9 said the cabinet had granted Foreign Min. Francisco San Tiago Dantas' request for the continuation of ex-Pres. Quadros' foreign policy of improving Brazilian relations with Communist countries and of keeping "hands off" Cuba. (A Foreign Ministry spokesman said this policy would be practiced without "petty, aggressive gestures toward" the U.S.) The communique also said there would be "no modification" of Quadros' economic and financial policies or of the coffee policy.

In an interview following a cabinet meeting Sept. 10, Dantas said Brazil would "pursue" an "independent" course that "will sometimes lead into an alignment with the Soviet bloc, with the neutralists or with the Western bloc, in each case in terms of how world peace can best be served." He said Brazil would "spare no effort to maintain" Cuba's Castro regime "within the inter-American system ..." Dantas announced that Brazilian-USSR negotiations to reestablish diplomatic relations, suspended Aug. 29, would be resumed.

Soviet Relations Resumed

Foreign Min. Dantas informed the Chamber of Deputies Nov. 23 that Brazil and the Soviet Union had resumed diplomatic relations. Notes renewing the ties, which had been severed by Brazil in 1947, were signed Nov. 23 by Dantas and Victor Azov, head of a permanent USSR trade mission in Brasilia. Anti-Communist deputies jeered Dantas as he made his announcement.

Dantas explained Nov. 25 that Brazil had renewed relations with the USSR "but not with communism." The move, he said, would provide political and economic benefits for Brazil. Premier Tancredo Neves insisted the same day that "we continue being a Christian, democratic nation."

The USSR had been wooing Brazil assiduously in an effort to reestablish the diplomatic ties. Finally, Janio Quadros, while still president, had announced at a news conference in Brasilia July 25 that he had instructed his Foreign Ministry to resume diplomatic relations with the USSR. Afonso Arinos de Melo Franco, Brazilian foreign minister at that time, had told members of a visiting Soviet goodwill mission July 24 that Brazil hoped to establish such relations shortly and to increase trade with the USSR.

The USSR's acceptance of Vasco Leitao da Cunha as Brazilian ambassador to the Soviet Union was made public Dec. 2.

Economic Developments

After Quadros' resignation, the new premier, Tancredo Neves, submitted to Congress Sept. 28 a program for social reform and industrial development with financial stability. Reporting that the program was based largely on Quadros' policies, Neves said: "The over-all price level in Brazil ..., starting from a base of 100 in 1947, reached an index of 739 by 1960. This sharp inflation had its foreseeable consequences in that it discouraged personal savings, impaired large long-term investments, caused an imbalance in the balance of payments, diverted funds to nonproductive activities. Worst of all, it gave rise to social disturbances because, while a small group of persons got richer, the inflation caused painful difficulties for the great mass of the Brazilian population—especially those in the lower income brackets, whose wages were daily eaten away by rising prices."

Neves listed these tasks for the new government: wage adjustments; agrarian reform; industrial development; regulation of profit remittances abroad; anti-trust legislation; banking, fiscal and monetary reforms, and legislation to improve educational and literacy levels.

The Chamber of Deputies approved Neves' economic program by 174-to-11 vote (with 141 abstentions) Sept. 29.

Neves Nov. 14 submitted to Congress a tax reform bill and proposed an anti-inflationary program that called for budget-deficit reduction, bank reforms, credit-and-wage controls and production incentives. Brazil had to have basic structural changes and not just monetary and currency-exchange modifications, Neves said.

Before adjourning in mid-December, Congress approved the Brazilian budget for 1962. Neves, addressing Congress Dec. 10, disclosed an anticipated deficit of 134.52 billion cruzeiros ($450 million), as compared with ex-Pres. Quadros' estimate in May of a 126.4 billion-cruzeiro deficit. Neves said Quadros' projection was based on an optimistic overestimate of revenues. Neves' budget called for 573.536 billion cruzeiros in expenditures. It anticipated revenues totaling 439.016 billion cruzeiros. Major items of expenditure included transport and public works (165.591 billion cruzeiros), the armed services (101.844 billion cruzeiros), finance (106.471 billion cruzeiros), education (48.552 billion cruzeiros), labor and social insurance (35.756 billion cruzeiros), health (24.772 billion cruzeiros), agriculture (22.553 billion cruzeiros).

The cost of living in Brazil rose by 43% in 1961. Brazil's legal minimum wage was raised by 40% Oct. 16 in a continuing effort to keep up with rising costs and to reduce poverty levels.

Labor trouble erupted again toward the end of the year. Dante Pelacani, head of the Industrial Workers' Confederation (CNTI), called a general strike for Dec. 14 in the city of Sao Paulo in an attempt to obtain wage increases to keep up with the price increases. Before the strike could begin, however, Gov. Carlos Carvalho Pinto of the state of Sao Paulo declared the strike illegal and subversive and used police to prevent it. Units of the Brazilian 2d Army were alerted, but the strike was already broken; more than 1,200 workers and several union leaders were arrested.

Private banks in 8 West European countries had agreed in Paris July 31 to lend the Bank of Brazil $110 million to enable Brazil to repay a $300 million debt it owed those nations. (The countries involved: Britain, Belgium, France, Italy, the Netherlands, Sweden, Switzerland and West Germany.) The loan, comprising 56 separate agreements, was negotiated by roving Brazilian Amb. Roberto de Oliveira Campos during a European trip 3 months previously. Campos had reached agreement with representatives of the 8 governments May 24 to consolidate Brazil's European debt.

The U.S.' new Agency for International Development (AID) lent Brazil $50 million Nov. 20. The loan agreement was signed in Washington Nov. 20 by Roberto Campos and Teodoro Moscoso, U.S. assistant foreign aid administrator for Latin America. The loan, the AID's first, was to finance essential imports and to help stabilize Brazil's economy. The funds also were to help repay a $30 million U.S. credit advanced to Brazil in October to help meet a balance-of-payments deficit.

The U.S. and the International Monetary Fund (IMF) had announced May 17 that they would lend Brazil $498 million to help ease balance-of-payments difficulties. The U.S. agreed to lend Brazil $338 million and permit it to delay repayment of a previous $305 million loan. The IMF agreed to provide Brazil with $160 million in stand-by credit ($40 million of which was to be repaid in 12 months) and to grant it a postponement of repayment of a $140 million debt. (Brazil's foreign debt currently totaled $2.859 billion, including $1.759 billion owed to the U.S.) As a condition of the U.S. and IMF aid, Brazil agreed to reduce its huge budget deficit, restrain private credit and drop its inflationary support of coffee exports.

Although the U.S. and the IMF had made it a prime condition of their mid-May loans that Brazil pledge to abandon its 5-year-old practice of granting inflationary subsidies for coffee exports, Brazil failed to implement this part of the agreement. Accordingly, Brazil enjoyed another big trading year in this commodity as far as export volume went. Value received, however, was quite another story—as these figures for Brazilian coffee exports show:

Year	Million Bags	Million U. S. $	AveragePrice Per Bag (U. S. $)	Per Cent of Total Value of Brazilian Exports
1957	14.32	845.5	59.04	60.76
1958	12.88	687.5	53.36	55.31
1959	17.44	733.0	42.04	57.18
1960	16.82	712.7	42.37	56.17
1961	16.97	710.4	41.85	50.63

Imports were reduced by Brazil from a total value of $1.463 billion in 1960 to $1.426 billion in 1961. Total imports from the U.S. rose from a value of $443 million in 1960 to $515 million in 1961, but the economic aid portion of the totals amounted to $83 million in 1960 and $299 million in 1961.

Leftist Movements

The formation of a National Liberation Front to promote nationalist and leftist goals was made public Oct. 25 by Gov. Leonel Brizola of Rio Grande do Sul State at a rally in Goiania, capital of Goias State. The movement, formed by politicians who had supported Goulart's succession to the presidency in September, included Brizola, Gov. Mauro Borges of Goias State and Deputy Jose Joffily. A formal declaration by the front opposed Brazil's subordination "to international plunder, especially by North American groups." It urged: (1) greater control of foreign capital in Brazil (such control to include the nationalization of deposits in foreign bank branches); (2) agrarian reform; (3) confiscation of "illicit fortunes."

Among the people in the chronically poor region of Brazil's Northeast there was developing, meanwhile, a spirit more militant than ever in recent memory. Francisco Juliao, organizer of the Ligas Campaneses (Peasant Leagues, or rural unions), told an interviewer that he doubted whether a Congress swayed "by conservatives and landowners" would adopt the legislation needed to realize the sweeping land reforms that Brazil, in his opinion, required. The *N.Y. Times* Nov. 12 quoted Juliao as warning that if the peasants could not gain land by legal means, they would take it by revolution.

Educational Reform

A long-debated bill reforming and decentralizing Brazil's education system was passed by Congress Dec. 21. The country's first general education law, this Law of Directives & Bases of National Education (*Lei de Diretizes e Bases de Educacao Nacional)* was designed to implement Article 168 of the 15-year-old Brazilian constitution of 1946.

The constitution had mandated: "Free, compulsory public elementary education, with instruction in the Portuguese language; access to other levels of education without charge to those unable to pay the necessary fees; free elementary education provided by industrial, commercial, and agricultural enterprises, employing more than 100 persons, for children of their employes, and free apprentice training for minor employes; optional religious instruction as a part of regular study programs; teacher tenure [*catedratico*] rights and competitive examinations for positions in public secondary and public or free higher education institutions." (Although the 1966 constitution did not sustain lifetime tenure, professors who had tenure when the 1966 charter took effect continued to have tenure.)

The new law gave the federal government responsibility for public education in the territories but delegated to the states the duty of setting up and administering state public education systems under federal guidelines.

1962

POLITICAL & ECONOMIC MALAISE

1962 was a year of political and economic uneasiness for Brazil. The parliamentary system created to weaken Joao Goulart's powers as president did not work adequately, and the economy appeared to be slowing as a result of political unrest. Goulart opposed the new parliamentary system, and the Brazilian military trusted neither the president nor the new form of government. Although the Congressional and gubernatorial elections in October revealed what was considered a general sense of political moderation in the electorate, sharp clashes in the Northeast indicated deepened tension in that area. Brazilian-U.S. relations deteriorated as a result of the expropriation of U.S.-owned public utility companies.

In 1962 the government tried to establish more modern ground rules for foreign investors. In a concession to ultra-nationalist elements, the Goulart administration permitted 2 states to expropriate foreign-owned public utilities, but it blocked a 3d proposed nationalization. Inflation continued, but the federal administration managed by the year's end to evolve a comprehensive economic plan for slowing the price increases and spurring domestic development. Brazil, meanwhile, went deeper into debt to foreign creditors.

Nationalizations Hit U.S.-Owned Utilities

Gov. Leonel da Moura Brizola of Rio Grande do Sul Feb. 16 ordered the expropriation of his state's U.S. owned phone system, the Companhia Telefonica Nacional, a subsidiary of the International Telephone & Telegraph (IT&T) Co. of New York. The takeover, "in the public interest," canceled the company's operating title and provided for the seizure of all its books and properties. The firm, which served the state capital, Porto Alegre, and the state's interior, valued its property at $6-$8 million. Brizola, Pres. Goulart's brother-in-law, reportedly deposited 149,758,000 cruzeiros (about $140,000) as indemnity for the company's assets. The seizure followed nearly 2 years of unsuccessful talks between Brizola and company officials for state purchase of the phone system. The talks had broken down about 6 months previously when Brizola rejected a company request for a rate increase to help it expand its facilities. As a result, Brizola had established a state-owned phone system to compete with the IT&T subsidiary.

The U.S. State Department said Feb. 17, in a statement criticizing the seizure: "We acknowledge the right of a government to expropriate property ... for public purposes if provision is made for the payment of ... adequate ... compensation. However, when a government expropriates existing resources or issues its own funds to buy out existing operations, rather than using those funds to create new wealth, new jobs and new taxpayers and to increase productivity, this action appears to be a step backward in the mobilization of available resources for the success of the Alliance for Progress." "The amount offered [for the seized company] obviously is so far below book value that the evaluation appears to have been made unilaterally."

U.S. Amb.-to-Brazil Lincoln Gordon discussed the seizure with Foreign Min. Francisco San Tiago Dantas in Rio de Janeiro Feb. 17. After the meeting, Gordon issued a statement in which he said that Brizola, "in response" to Goulart's "expressed desire" for "an amicable settlement," had agreed to discuss compensation payments "in a spirit of mutual understanding." Dantas reportedly had told Gordon that Brizola's seizure action did not reflect the Goulart administration's attitude toward foreign investments in Brazil. (Brizola previously had expropriated an American & Foreign Power subsidary and a Swift & Co. packing plant.)

Pressure began to develop on the U.S. government from the U.S. business community for formal action to protect U.S. private investments in Brazil. But U.S. Pres. John F. Kennedy said at his news conference in Washington Mar. 9 that it would be "unwise" for U.S. Congress members to adopt a hostile attitude toward Brazil because of Rio Grande do Sul's expropriation of the U.S.-owned phone system. Sen. Russell B. Long (D., La.) and Rep. E. Ross Adair (R., Ind.) the previous week had introduced bills to halt aid to any country seizing U.S. property. Long also had urged the President to halt all aid to Brazil. But Kennedy said: The company had been "seized by the governor of a province who has not always been identified particularly as a friend of" the U.S.; "we have been attempting to work out an equitable solution with" Brazil; "I can think of nothing more unwise than to attempt to pass a resolution at this time which puts us in a position not of disagreement with a governor ... who is not particularly our friend, but ... with the whole Brazilian nation, ... with which we must have the closest relations"; settlement of "this matter" "is in our interests and in the interests of Brazil"; "[Brazilian] Pres. Goulart is coming here in April, and we will be discussing any matters which involve our relations."

Brizola Mar. 12 rejected a U.S. embassy suggestion that the phone company seizure dispute be submitted to international arbitration. Brizola's stand was supported by many army officers. But Gen. Jose Segadas Viana, the war minister, held that one general had been too enthusiastic. Gen. Peri Constant Bevilacqua, commander of the 3d Military Region was placed under house arrest Mar. 15 for 48 hours for using "indelicate language" affecting Brazil's international relations in violation of the military code. The charge stemmed from a telegram Bevilacqua had sent Brizola. In his telegram Bevilacqua had praised Brizola for expropriating the U.S.-owned company. Alluding to a State Department contention that the expropriation could endanger the U.S.' Alliance for Progress program in Brazil, Bevilacqua said: "Assistance to under-developed countries should not be subordinated to limitations or conditions of any nature that can restrict ... sovereignty."

Gov. Carlos Lacerda of Guanabara moved Mar. 30 to expropriate the state's Canadian-owned Brazilian Telephone Co., a subsidiary of the Brazilian Traction, Light & Power Co. of Toronto. But Goulart Apr. 2 prevented the take-over. Lacerda's request for state court approval of the seizure was blocked by Goulart's appointment of Gen. Jair Dantas Ribeiro, First Army commander, as federal controller of the firm. Goulart and Premier Tancredo Neves Mar. 27 had issued a decree barring the expropriation of interstate telecommunication systems without the approval of the National Security Council and the public works minister.

Brazilian Traction Pres. Henry Borden said in Toronto that his firm had been negotiating to sell its assets to the federal government "for the purpose of its [the government's] forming the nucleus of a nationwide phone system." The company owned and operated about 80% of the phones in Brazil. It was the largest firm of its kind in the country. The Guanabara state government Mar. 21 had informed the firm and the federal government that the state would oppose the sale of the company's property in Guanabara.

Lacerda's Mar. 30 expropriation decree had been issued after a meeting in Rio de Janeiro that day with Borden, who estimated the value of the firm's assets at more than $60 million. Lacerda had said expropriation was justified on the ground that the company had failed to provide adequate service. He said that although the company had installed more than 300,000 phones in Rio de Janeiro, more than 200,000 applicants were still waiting for service. Lacerda had returned to Brazil earlier Mar. 30 from Washington, where he had conferred with Pres. Kennedy.

The Pernambuco state court in Recife seized the U.S.-owned Pernambuco Tramways & Power Co., Ltd. July 18 after company officials refused to surrender the firm without prior compensation. The company valued its property at $8-$12 million. State authorities had contended that the company's franchise provided for state ownership of the firm following the expiration of its 50-year contract earlier in the week. The state also had argued that the company had been compensated by a user's tax.

Goulart, addressing the U.S. Chamber of Commerce of Rio de Janeiro Mar. 23, had said that Brazil welcomed foreign capital but reserved the right to select those operations whose development did the most for Brazil's economy. He added that foreign-owned public utilities should be prepared to accept a just solution for the transfer of their holdings to Brazilian hands.

Goulart in U.S., Pledges Fairness

In an attempt to improve Brazilian-American relations, Pres. Goulart accepted an invitation to visit the U.S. Apr. 3-9, and pledged that foreign investors would be treated fairly— even if Brazil decided to expropriate their property.

Pres. Kennedy greeted Goulart as he arrived in Washington by plane Apr. 3. The 2 presidents conferred Apr. 3-4 and then issued a joint communique that said:

"... Political democracy, national independence and self determination, and the liberty of the individual are the political principles which shape" the national policies of Brazil and the U.S. The 2 presidents would "continue to work to reduce world tensions through negotiations insuring progressive disarmament under effective controls." They "reaffirmed the dedication of their countries to the inter-American system" and expressed their intention to ... work together to protect this hemisphere against all forms of aggression." "The presidents reaffirmed their adherence to the principles of the charter of Punta del Este." They "agreed on the need for rapid execution of the steps necessary to make the Alliance for Progress effective." Goulart expressed Brazil's "intention" "to strengthen the machinery for national programming, selection of priorities and preparation of projects." Mr. Kennedy "indicated the readiness of the [U.S.] to assign representatives to work closely with such Brazilian agencies to minimize delays in project selection and the provision of external support." The 2 presidents "expressed hope" that U.S. assistance to Brazil's program for the development of Brazil's poverty-stricken Northeast would provide a fruitful response at an early date." Goulart stated his government's "intention" "to maintain conditions of security which will permit private capital to perform its vital role" in Brazil; he pledged that "in arrangements with the [private] companies for the transfer of public utility enterprises to Brazilian ownership the principle of fair compensation ... would be maintained." The presidents indicated their support of the "Latin American Free Trade Area" "to promote the expansion of Latin American markets." They "restated their conviction that the destiny of the hemisphere lay in the collaboration of nations united in faith in individual liberty, free institutions and human dignity."

White House Press Secy. Pierre Salinger said after the conferences that Kennedy had accepted Goulart's invitation to visit Brazil "this year."

In an address before a joint session of the U.S. Congress Apr. 4, Goulart declared that Brazil adhered to "the democratic principles which united the peoples of the West" but was "not part of any politico-military bloc." Goulart lauded the Kennedy Administration for having created the Alliance for Progress. Goulart asserted that Brazil would maintain its traditionally close ties with the West but keep an independent stance on some international developments. He said:

Brazil's international action responds to no other objective than that of assisting, by all means in her power, in the preservation and strengthening of peace.... Brazil believes that a noninimical contact between the democratic world and the Socialist world can be beneficial to knowledge and coordination of experience. It is our hope that these contacts will make it evident that representative democracy is the most perfect of all forms of government and the only one compatible with the protection of mankind and the preservation of human freedom.

In his speech before Congress Goulart acknowledged Brazil's need for financial aid and development capital. He traced many of his country's economic problems back to the trade dislocations of World War II. Goulart said:

The Latin American countries, with their war-born inflation, remained devoid of any international cooperation for the recovery of their agriculture and the development of their industries, and counted only on the export of their primary products for the restoration of their trade. The growing deterioration of the terms of trade of primary products compared with manufactured goods is well known to all. From year to year, the same number of bags of coffee or of cocoa or of cotton buys an ever lesser quantity of the same type of equipment or of manufactured products. While our primary products have remained exposed to a continued fall in prices, our population has increased at such a rate that Brazil is expected to possess 200 million inhabitants at the end of this century....

We desire [foreign technical] cooperation and will assure its full freedom within the legal limits established and under the inspiration of Brazilian ideals.... As a country now in a phase of full expansion, Brazil offers broad possibilities to foreign private enterprise desirous of cooperating loyally for its development. In the matter of public utilities services, there are certain areas of friction which it is convenient to eliminate....

But as for the long-awaited program of Pan American economic aid and cooperation, which Goulart likened to the postwar Marshall Plan in Western Europe in its scope, he still had some reservations. He declared:

... I cannot conceal, however, my fears as to the difficulties of execution. If the Alliance for Progress is to depend upon an effort by the Latin American countries to achieve global planning with absolute technical precision in the economic and social fields, and to eliminate beforehand certain factors of instability, we can introduce hindrances capable of impairing the urgency of solutions which cannot be put off. Such difficulties will mount if the Alliance fails to reflect the spirit of reciprocal trust and respect between the countries which comprise it, in line with the purposes expressed by the eminent Pres. Kennedy.

Goulart went to New York Apr. 5-6 as the guest of Mayor Robert Wagner, lunched with UN Secy. Gen. U Thant Apr. 6 and held a press conference, at UN headquarters, at which he disclosed plans for further utilities nationalizations. He met U.S. Amb.-to-UN Adlai Stevenson and Gov. Nelson Rockefeller of New York and spoke at a special banquet sponsored by 3 groups, at which he outlined Brazil's stance toward foreign capital. At his press conference Goulart said that Brazil would give "every freedom and every guarantee" of fair profits to investors whose properties had been or would be expropriated in Brazil. Foreign-owned utilities in Brazil could no longer provide "the great services they had rendered in the past," Goulart declared. He said such utilities had become "friction centers" that eventually injured relations between Brazil and the countries in which their owners resided.

Goulart visited the U.S. Strategic Air Command headquarters in Omaha, Neb. Apr. 7, then went to Chicago. He left the U.S. Apr. 9 and arrived in Mexico City later that day for a state visit before returning to Brazil.

Mexican Visit Cut Short

As the first Brazilian head of state to visit Mexico, Goulart received an enthusiastic welcome Apr. 9 from large crowds along the route into Mexico City from its airport. Mexican Pres. Alfonso Lopez Mateos received Goulart, and the 2 leaders began talks immediately. But before Goulart could complete his planned itinerary, he returned to Brazil Apr. 11 because of what was described as a sudden illness.

The 2 Latin American presidents issued a joint communique in which they stressed the independent and essentially nonaligned character of Brazilian and Mexican foreign policy philosophies. They again reassured each other's countrymen and the world that both lands would observe faithfully all treaties and agreements already undertaken.

Policy on Foreign-Owned Firms & Nationalization

The Brazilian government late in May formally adopted a new position on the proper scope of foreign investors' operations within Brazil. The Council of Ministers (cabinet) May 23 approved a decree (Decree No. 1106) setting forth the procedure under which all major public services, particularly foreign-owned phone and power companies, were to be nationalized. A government spokesman said the measure "should not signify a reduction of foreign investment or serve to create a climate of inhibiting new investment." Under the decree, signed by Goulart May 24 and issued May 30, a 3-man commission, directly responsible to the Council of Ministers, would negotiate with each public utility the terms on which the government planned to nationalize its properties. The maximum initial payment the government would make for a seized enterprise would be 10% of the property's value. The nationalized firm would be obliged to make a long-term investment in Brazil of at least 75% of the total payment received. This reinvestment would have to be in areas designated as important to Brazil's economic development. The price offered to nationalized firms would be subject to arbitration, and the Supreme Court president would be final arbiter. (The nationalization commission went into operation June 18.)

In another victory for Brazilian nationalist elements, as political strife over the parliamentary system intensified, Congress approved a new economic weapon designed to limit foreign exploitation. Goulart, expressing some reservations, signed into law Sept. 3 a bill giving the Superintendency of Currency & Credit control over foreign investments. Article 31 of this Law No. 4131 stipulated that "annual remittances abroad of profits may not exceed 10% of the registered value of the investment"; under Article 32, anything further "will be considered as repatriation of capital and deducted from the [capital's] registered value, thus affecting future remittances abroad of profits." Brazil henceforth would tax such firms' profits, interest and dividends in inverse ratio to the investment's importance to the Brazilian national economy.

Before the final enactment of Law No. 4131, U.S. Amb.-to-Brazil Lincoln Gordon, in a speech in Belem (Para State), had warned the Brazilian government that the bill's passage would discourage foreign investors at the time of Brazil's greatest need of outside capital for domestic development. Gov. Leonel Brizola of Rio Grande do Sul denounced Gordon as a meddler.

Foreign Aid

Despite the nationalization of U.S.-owned property in Rio Grande do Sul, the U.S. government Mar. 15 had concluded its 4th surplus wheat sales agreement with Brazil. The sale, made possible by the U.S. Agricultural Trade Development & Assistance Act of 1954 (PL 83-480), provided Brazil with 800,000 tons of wheat and 300,000 tons of corn. Under U.S. surplus-commodity sale procedures, Brazil paid for the wheat in cruzeiros ("counterpart" currency), which remained in Brazil and were used for a variety of aid projects mutually acceptable to the Brazilian and U.S. governments. It was estimated that the agreement thus generated more than $40 million in Alliance for Progress development aid in Brazil.

A U.S. grant of 850 million cruzeiros in such counterpart funds was made Feb. 27 to pro-U.S. Gov. Carlos Lacerda of Guanabara to improve water and sewage services in Rio de Janeiro and to carry out improvements in the *favelas* (slums).

A fresh wheat sales agreement was signed by the U.S. and Brazil Oct. 4. This agreement provided for the shipment of 600,000 tons of U.S. grain, valued at $43 million, to Brazil. Repayment was to be made over a 40-year period.

U.S. aid to Brazil amounted to $715 million in grants between Dec. 1960 and Apr. 13, 1962, when the U.S. and Brazil signed new Alliance for Progress agreements under which the U.S. and Brazil provided a total of $276 million for the development of Brazil's Northeast. Of the $715 million granted by the U.S., $354 million had already been allocated by April—and $209 million of that subtotal had been drawn for use as currency stabilization credits.

The U.S. embassy in Rio de Janeiro disclosed in October the following distribution of more than $636½ million in U.S. aid in Brazil: Currency stabilization and essential imports, $254 million; funds for development (from surplus wheat sales),

$140.2 million; development aid for Northeast, $134.4 million; Food-for-Peace distribution, $36.2 million; technical assistance (antimalaria campaign), $15.8 million; Social Progress Fund assistance, $55.9 million.

While Pres. Goulart was away visiting the U.S., the Brazilian government was informed Apr. 4 that the International Monetary Fund had decided to postpone Brazil's obligation to repurchase $20 million it had drawn from the Fund.

Northeast: the Major Trouble Area

The deteriorating economic situation in Brazil's overwhelmingly agricultural Northeast Region, made even worse by drought, had arrived at the danger point and had attracted the entire hemisphere's attention before Goulart took office as president in Sept. 1961. The region, comprising the states of Maranhao, Piaui, Ceara, Rio Grande do Norte, Paraiba, Pernambuco, Alagoas, Sergipe and Bahia, make up just over 15% of Brazil's total area (approximately 600,000 square miles) and is larger than Italy, Spain and Portugal combined. 31% of the country's total population, approximately 25 million, lived in the area at the beginning of the decade.

Early in 1961, Janio Quadros, then president, had made public a 1958 report, drawn up by a group of army investigators during the height of the long drought but suppressed by his predecessor, Juscelino Kubitschek, that disclosed unacceptably poor living conditions. "It is no longer necessary for us to read the histories of China and India to know the significance and extent of misery," the investigators had concluded. "Right here in Brazil there is at this moment a population living on the lowest standard of subnutrition that a people can endure."

About the time that Quadros had revealed this report, the new U.S. Administration, planning the Alliance for Progress, had shown increased concern for the poverty-stricken area. Pres. John F. Kennedy dispatched George McGovern, U.S. Food-for-Peace director, and Presidential Asst. Arthur Schlesinger Jr. on a tour of the area. After learning their findings, the Kennedy Administration had indorsed the $10 million loan made Feb. 27, 1961 by the Inter-American Development Bank for agricultural and industrial improvements in the region.

Other countries in the hemisphere also expressed their desire to aid the region. Cuba's interest in the area, however, caused serious concern in the U.S., whose government indicated fear that Cuba was trying to foment popular unrest in some of the 8 Northeast states.

CAMPONESAS

The Northeast, meanwhile, had sprouted a social reform movement of its own, the *Ligas Campaneses* (Peasant Leagues), whose mission was to campaign for tenant security and agrarian reform. Reports of violent activities attributed to the Peasant Leagues had been relayed from the region as early as the summer of 1960. The leagues had been founded by Deputy Francisco Juliao, president of the Pernambuco chapter of the Socialist Party. Tad Szulc had reported in the *N.Y. Times* Nov. 1, 1960 that "the leaders of the league[s] insist that it is a cooperative movement operating in the absence of trade unions for rural workers in Brazil and designed to represent the illiterate peasants in land-tenancy court cases. But they freely concede that its broader objective is to make the Northeastern population a powerful political force." Szulc said that the league(s) were "led by officials of the Brazilian Socialist Party, who acknowledge their Marxist leanings, and by members of the Communist Party." He reported that, publicly, league leaders had warned that "if need be, they will urge an agrarian revolution," whereas "in private conversation many have said that a revolution is inevitable" before long. In a manifesto published in the Communist weekly *Novos Rumos* in Rio de Janeiro and circulated throughout the Northeast in Oct. 1960, Juliao assured his followers: "Your cruel enemy, the *latifundium* [big estate], will die as it died in China ... [and] as it died in Cuba, where the great Fidel Castro handed a rifle to each peasant and said: "Democracy is the government that arms the people." I went there and saw it all."

Early in Apr. 1962, while Pres. Goulart was away in Washington, D.C., the assassination of a Northeast league leader pointed up the increasing polarization of emotions in the region and signaled a new phase in the crisis. Joao Pedro Teixeira, 39, acting president of the Peasant League of Sape in the state of Paraiba was shot to death Apr. 3. Sape peasants planning a protest march on Joao Pessoa, Paraiba's capital, were blocked by soldiers Apr. 9-10. Paraiba police chief Francisco Maria Junio said Apr. 10 that 2 rural policemen had been arrested, and a 3d suspect was sought, as Teixeira's assassins. The police said that the suspects had been hired by landholders to murder Teixeira in reprisal for an attack by peasants in February on Pedro Ramos' Miriri ranch, near Sape, where 1,000 families worked as tenants. The ranch manager, a 2d employe and a tenant were killed in the fighting. The Peasant League of Sape was one of Paraiba's 8 peasant leagues (total membership: about 12,000). (The Federation of Peasant Leagues in Paraiba was headed by Prof. Assis Lemos of the Paraiba University School of Agronomy.)

As the drought in the Northeast's interior reached disaster proportions, farmers began to abandon their land and to stream into the small towns in search of food and employment. Celso Furtado, director of the Superintendency for the Development of the Northeast (SUDENE), estimated by May that 500,000 people were affected, at least 240,000 of them in the state of Pernambuco. Political infighting among Brazilian agencies was in evidence as the Federal Drought Agency (DNOCS) accused the SUDENE of withholding quantities of U.S. aid.

The rural movement meetings, which at first had been small and local, began to grow in size and in the areas represented. The First Congress of Farmers & Rural Workers of the North & Northeast was held in Itabuna, Bahia May 10-13. One of the organizers was the Rev. Antonio Melo Costa, 28, a Roman Catholic priest from Cabo, Pernambuco, and the first priest known to become publicly involved in the movement.

Pres. Goulart Aug. 1 opened the first national congress of the Federations of Farm Leagues in Joao Pessoa, capital of Paraiba. In his speech before 15,000 delegates, Goulart noted a need for an "authentically national" agrarian reform movement and declared that development in the Northeast should be based on: (1) the creation of an economic infra-structure; (2) a study of the natural resources of the region, and (3) an increase in private investment in the area.

U.S. & Brazil Share Northeast Aid Costs

A U.S.-Brazilian agreement to commit $276 million in Alliance for Progress funds for Brazil's Northeast Region was signed in Washington Apr. 13 by U.S. State Secy. Dean Rusk and Brazilian Foreign Min. Francisco San Tiago Dantas. The U.S.' Agency for International Development was to provide

$131 million, Brazil $145 million. The funds were to be used for such projects as the creation of pure-water supplies, rural electrification, school construction, irrigation, electric power development, road improvement and education. U.S. Pres. Kennedy Apr. 13 made public a letter in which he told Brazilian Pres. Goulart: "We approach this program with the same sense of urgency ... that your government has demonstrated in its planning for this region"; "we share with you the conviction that the 20 million people in the Northeast must be afforded an opportunity to participate in the future growth of Brazil."

The federal government May 11 announced a food emergency in the drought-stricken area (which included a small part of Minas Gerais). Special measures to speed food to the famine-stricken sections were adopted by the SUDENE Council, the federal agency through which U.S. financial and food aid was being channeled. UN food donations also were being rushed to the area. (Leonard Wolff, U.S. Food-for-Peace director in Brazil, announced in Rio de Janeiro May 13, after visiting the Northeast, that 10,000 tons of U.S. surplus beans had been ordered shipped to the area. Some of the 8,000 tons of Food-for-Peace corn stored in Recife and Bahia, 2 principal Northeast cities, were ordered released.) The food crisis had been further heightened by the failure of the manioc crop in southern Brazil; manioc was used in the Northeast for manioc flour, a staple. Food prices in the Northeast had gone up sharply since Jan. 1; the cost of some foods had risen as much as 300%.

The government also announced an emergency public works program to employ persons idled by the drought. The first program approved was for $2½ million in road and water reservoir projects in the states of Pernambuco and Paraiba; the projects were to employ 13,000 men in communities where rainfall during the current planting season had been less than 50% of normal. More than 15,000 unemployed already had been put to work on federal and state projects in the state of Bahia, where, according to officials, 90% of the bean and corn crops had been destroyed by the dry weather. The drought had spread from the interior of Bahia north through western Pernambuco and southwestern Paraiba.

2 U.S. Alliance for Progress agreements providing aid for the Northeast were signed in Recife June 4 by U.S. Amb.-to-Brazil Lincoln Gordon and Brazilian officials. One agreement was for a water system for 140 communities at a cost of about $17 million over a 2-year period; the other would provide health stations at a cost of $3 million in addition to 175 million cruzeiros ($437,000) received from the sale of U.S. wheat in Brazil.

Quadros Returns to Brazil

Ex-Pres. Janio da Silva Quadros, 45, had returned to Brazil Mar. 7. He had traveled abroad for 6 months after resigning the presidency. More than 10,000 enthusiastic supporters, according to wire services' estimates, waited near the dockside in Santos to welcome Quadros. Gov. Jose de Magalhaes Pinto of Minas Gerias and representatives of Govs. Leonel Brizola of Rio Grande do Sul and Carlos Carvalho Pinto of Sao Paulo were also on hand.

In a statement at the dock, Quadros declared: "I return to fight, whatever the cost, for the republic about which we dream.... There is only one solution: we must stay united.... And woe to those who want to know, and who do not belong to the people, the reasons for my renouncing the presidency. The reasons for my renunciation will be known in the public squares."

In a nationwide TV-radio address Mar. 15, Quadros explained his resignation as president. Quadros said: His withdrawal had been precipitated by the decision of a group of Congressmen to investigate Guanabara Gov. Carlos Lacerda's charges that Quadros was conspiring to adjourn Congress and rule by decree; the purpose of Lacerda's charges and the proposed probe was to "destroy the executive power"; to openly oppose Congress would have placed Brazil "one step away from the destruction" of its constitutional government; the Aug. 1961 crisis had resulted from opposition to economic reforms; this opposition came from leftist and rightist forces "or economic forces and the Communists" in Congress.

Quadros charged these 3 U.S. officials with having hampered his regime: ex-U.S. Amb.-to-Brazil John Moors Cabot, who was accused by Quadros of "unfitting interference in Brazil's affairs"; Adolf A. Berle Jr., U.S. Pres. Kennedy's ex-Latin American affairs adviser, who had purportedly proposed to Quadros that the American republics take "political, economic and even military" action against Cuba; U.S. Treasury Secy. Douglas Dillon, who had allegedly sought to mix foreign policy with Brazil's need for foreign credit. Quadros also denounced ex-West German Amb. Herbert Dittman, who had shown "irritation" at a Brazilian trade mission's 1961 visit to East Germany.

Quadros announced that his political plans called for leading "a people's crusade" against the "reactionaries, the corrupt and the Communists."

Friendliness to Cuba & Ties to USSR

The Goulart administration continued its friendly relationship with Cuba. Foreign Min. Francisco San Tiago Dantas Feb. 7 defended his delegation's decision to abstain in voting in Punta del Este on an OAS (Organization of American States) foreign ministers' resolution excluding Cuba from the inter-American system.

Dantas said in a report to the Chamber of Deputies: "It is not true that Cuba is lost as a nation for coexistence with the other countries of the hemisphere"; other American republics should seek a negotiated arrangement with Cuba; Brazil should continue its policy "of peace and of seeking a road to negotiations"; that policy could not be considered as favoring communism since Brazil had joined the other American republics at Punta del Este in voting for the resolution that declared communism incompatible with the principles of the inter-American system; U.S. State Secy. Dean Rusk had not tried to exert economic pressure against Brazil and the 5 other American nations that had abstained in voting on the Cuban exclusion resolution.

Dantas charged that "powerful forces were at work in Brazil promoting acts of terrorism." In reply to a deputy's demand that he identify the "powerful forces," Dantas said it was up to the justice minister to supply such information. (Recent "acts of terrorism" apparently referred to by Dantas: the USSR's commercial office in Rio de Janeiro was bombed; the left-wing National Student Union headquarters was the target of bullets from a passing car.)

The Castro regime, however, had some strong enemies in Brazil. An anti-Castro Cuban exile group Feb. 11 claimed the support of Gov. Carlos Lacerda of Guanabara State, who was, perhaps, politically the most powerful civilian outside the federal administration in Brazil. Jose Miro Cardona, the first premier in Castro's administration and later chairman of the exiles' Cuban Revolutionary Council, listed Lacerda's name among the names of leading or prominent Latin Americans who supported a new hemispherewide anti-Communist alliance against Castro.

Soviet Amb.-to-Brazil Ilya Semyonovich Chernyshev presented his credentials to Goulart Feb. 28 as the Soviet Union's first ambassador to Brazil in about 15 years. All ties between Brazil and the USSR had been severed in 1947 after the Kremlin had rejected requests from the Dutra administration for an apology for alleged Soviet press insults to the Brazilian army.

Congressional forces of the right attempted unsuccessfully in May to censure the Goulart administration for its "independent" foreign policy operations.

The Chamber of Deputies May 30, by 131-44 vote, defeated a Democratic Action Front motion to censure Dantas for his conduct of foreign policy. The front, an inter-party bloc representing rightists in the chamber, was critical of (a) Brazil's abstention in the OAS foreign ministers' vote excluding Cuba from the inter-American system at the Punta del Este conference in January and (b) Brazil's reestablishment of diplomatic relations with the USSR. A front leader, Deputy Dirceu Cardoso, charged that Dantas' policies were weakening resistance to the "establishment of communism in Brazil."

Cabinet Crisis

Brazil was plunged into a political and administrative crisis June 26 when Premier Tancredo de Almeida Neves and most of his cabinet resigned to run for Congress in the Oct. 7 elections.

(Neves, in a farewell speech in the Chamber of Deputies June 26, reviewed his 10 months in office and asserted that he had produced a comprehensive plan to control inflation through tax reform. It also had been necessary to raise salaries of civil and military personnel, Neves said. These salary increases had caused a rise in the budget deficit from 200 billion cruzeiros in Nov. 1961 to 330 billion in Apr. 1962.)

In a move to discredit and weaken the new parliamentary system, Goulart selected Francisco San Tiago Dantas as his new premier. Dantas, foreign minister in the Neves cabinet, was a strong proponent of the idea of an independent foreign policy such as would favor closer ties with the Soviet Union and the Communist bloc. Dantas appealed to the country's labor unions for support and attacked the *"status quo"* politicians of all parties.

The Chamber of Deputies, fearing Dantas' nomination as a threat to Congress' ascendancy, refused June 28, by 174-110 vote, to confirm him as premier. The 7-year-old coalition of Social Democrats and Brazilian Laborites split over the issue, conservative Social Democrats joining members of the National Democratic Union in opposition to Dantas, a Brazilian Laborite, as premier.

Goulart's next nominee, Senate Pres. Auro Soares de Mouro Andrade, 46, a Social Democrat from Sao Paulo, was approved by the Chamber of Deputies as premier July 2 by 222-51 vote.

But differences developed quickly between Goulart and the new premier over cabinet appointments and various policies. The labor unions backed the president, and Mouro Andrade resigned July 4. In an interview July 6, Mouro Andrade said that he had withdrawn because leaders of the major parties had rejected the military ministers whom he and Goulart had chosen.

A new labor group called the *Comando General dos Trabalhadores* (CGT, or General Workers' Command), claiming to be the legitimate heirs of the old Confederation of Brazilian Workers, scheduled one-day general strikes in Brazil's 5 major eastern port cities to rally support for Goulart and put pressure on Congress.

The political crisis had been intensified by food riots in 3 Rio de Janeiro suburbs July 5-6. The food shortage was caused by government efforts to control prices to combat inflation. At least 10 persons were killed in the disorders. The rioting occurred as leftist unions, supporting Goulart, staged a one-day general strike July 5-6 in a demand for the establishment of a "popular nationalist government." The walkout affected the major port cities of Rio de Janeiro, Recife, Porto Alegre, Santos and Fortaleza. The rioting erupted in and around Duque de Caxias (Rio de Janeiro State) July 5 when residents, angered by food shortages, sacked more than 50 grocery stores and butcher shops and set several afire. At least 6 persons were killed and more than 100 injured in clashes between the looters and merchants before troops restored order. 2 persons were killed in the neighboring town of Sao Joao de Meriti in similar rioting. 2 persons reportedly were killed July 6 as food stores were looted in Duque de Caxias. Looters also attacked stores and homes in the suburb of Nova Iguacu. Many Rio de Janeiro merchants closed their shops July 6 for fear of looting.

With the country reported to be on the verge of political and administrative collapse, Goulart selected Dr. Francisco Brochado da Rocha, a relatively obscure lawyer and justice minister for the state of Rio Grande do Sul, as his 3d candidate for the post of premier. A weary Chamber of Deputies confirmed his nomination July 10 by 215-58 vote. Most of the Congressmen of the Social Democratic, Brazilian Labor, Progressive Socialist, Republican, Brazilian Socialist and National Labor parties voted for Brochado da Rocha. Voting against him were the majority of the UDN and dissident PSP members.

Brochado da Rocha's new cabinet was seated July 13 after its acceptance by 139-63 vote. The cabinet: Foreign Affairs—Afonso Arinos de Melo Franco, Finance—Walter Moreira Salles; Justice—Candido de Oliveira Netto; War—Gen. Nelson de Melo; Air—Brig. Joaquim Reinaldo de Carvalho; Navy—Adm. Pedro Paul de Araujo Suzano; Labor—Prof. Hermes Lima; Mines & Energy—Joao Mangaveira; Agriculture—Renato da Costa Lima; Education—Helio de Almeida. But 2 nominees refused to serve; they were Jose Ermiro de Morais, named industry and commerce minister, and Dr. Marcelino Candau, named health minister.

Political & Diplomatic Uncertainty

The unsettled Brazilian political situation in the first half of July generated rumors of violence and had a generally discouraging effect on diplomacy for the time being. According to one report issuing from Congress, Goulart allegedly planned to close Congress and, with military support, arrange a plebiscite on the issue of ministerial responsibility to Congress.

In Washington, the White House announced July 12 that U.S. Pres. Kennedy's trip to Brazil, originally scheduled for July 30, had been postponed until Nov. 12 because Kennedy was needed in Washington during the closing period of the Congressional session and because Congressional elections were to be held in Brazil Oct. 7 and in the U.S. Nov. 6. Observers said an unannounced reason for the delay was the cabinet crisis in Brazil. Kennedy had conferred with Goulart by phone July 11, but the postponement was not announced until after White House Press Secy. Pierre Salinger arrived in Brasilia July 12, spoke with Goulart and then phoned Kennedy.

A new political trend became obvious in July when Gov. Leonel Brizola of Rio Grande do Sul and the Brazilian Socialists (PSB) agreed to form a left-wing popular front in anticipation of the October elections. Brizola pledged to deliver the support of Brazilian Laborites (PTB) under his influence or control. He named ex-Foreign Min. Francisco San Tiago Dantas to lead the new coalition in the Rio de Janeiro-Sao Paulo area. Mayor Miguel Arraes de Alencar of Recife, candidate for governor of Pernambuco, was chosen to head the organization in the Northeast.

Goulart Seeks More Power

Goulart, his political prestige enhanced by his trip to North America, had opened a political offensive in May in an effort to free his office of the constitutional limitations imposed on it by the federal congress late in the summer of 1961.

Goulart, addressing workers May 1 in the steel city of Volta Redonda, demanded a reform of Brazil's political system to enable the restoration of effective government. He charged that Congress was not dealing swiftly enough with the problems of agrarian reform, reform of the banking system and regulation of the remittance abroad of profits gained by foreign firms in Brazil. Goulart asserted that Brazil needed a regime that would ensure administrative efficiency and responsibility not to Congress but to the real interests of Brazilians generally. Such an administration, he added, must respect the popular will.

In a speech in the Sao Paulo State port city of Santos May 13, Goulart complained that under the current constitution, land reform became financially impossible. He also attacked the taxation system. Goulart said: "In Brazil, those who make the largest profits are often those who pay the least into the national treasury. We must also have a complete and systematic reorganization of our revenue collection system so that all shall pay a tax in proportion to their profits...."

Goulart proclaimed his support for a bill, then before Congress, to give the federal legislators elected in the Oct. 7 contest the right to amend the 1946 constitution and, by implication, the adjustments in it made in Sept. 1961.

Another extensive high-level political struggle began in August over the 11-month-old constitutional changes in government as Goulart appeared to be mounting his strongest drive yet to regain power. He made his move soon after Brazil's Supreme Electoral Court July 25 had declared itself incompetent to schedule a national plebiscite sought by Goulart to restore full executive powers to the presidency.

Premier Francisco Brochado da Rocha submitted to Congress Aug. 10 a petition requesting permission for his cabinet to rule by decree to cope with rising economic problems. Brochado also submitted an accompanying draft law proposed by Goulart that would empower the Supreme Electoral Court to call a national plebiscite by Dec. 20 to decide whether to replace the parliamentary system with a presidential form of government. Brochado's request for sweeping economic powers was embodied in a 22-point program that called for: (a) agricultural support prices and federal farm and livestock credits to increase farm output; (b) a labor law for rural workers, regulation of land rentals and sharecropping, expropriation of uneconomically tilled land and centralization of agrarian reform in one agency; (c) measures against "floundering" and "abuses of economic power," including laws that would "discipline" foreign investment and regulate the remittance of earnings abroad by foreign companies; (d) laws to give the government relative immunity against injunctions and greater control of national police services; (e) tax reforms, budget and federal accounting system reorganization and the strengthening of special funds for high-priority state investment.

Conservative forces in Congress opposed Brochado's request and sought to block passage of the proposals. Many leftist and nationalist Congressmen, however, favored such legislation. 2 Congressional committees in mid-August issued reports indorsing some of Brochado's proposals, but Congress itself failed to act during August on the request that decree powers be granted to the cabinet.

As Congress continued discussing Brochado's proposals well into September, Gen. Jair Dantas Ribeiro, commander of the 3d Army, stationed in Porto Alegre, wired a warning Sept. 12 to Goulart, Brochado and Gen. Nelson de Melo, the war minister. He asserted that he would "not be in a condition to maintain order" in the 3 states under his command (Parana, Santa Catarina and Rio Grande do Sul) unless Congress scheduled a plebiscite on the question of the parliamentary system for Oct. 7, election day.

War Min. Nelson de Melo, presumably taking the telegram as a challenge to his authority, answered immediately and counseled Ribeiro against the imprudence of defiance. Nelson de Melo told Ribeiro in his message:

> A solution to the problem [of continued ministerial responsibility] is being sought among the Council of Ministers [cabinet], the president of the republic and the national Congress with the noble desire of finding a formula that will terminate the institutional crisis. Only I, as head of the army and member of the Council of Ministers, am competent to give an opinion on this matter. Manifestations of this nature coming from subordinate [military] levels are not conducive to discipline. With regard to the question of public order in the area under your jurisdiction, I judge that your excellency is in a condition to maintain it.

Brochado's Resignation & Death

Premier Brochado put the parliamentary issue before the cabinet, which refused to authorize him to seek a Congressional vote of confidence. Brochado had staked everything on his proposal that Congress empower the Supreme Electoral Court to schedule a plebiscite on the constitutional issue for Oct. 7.

Brochado, 52, resigned Sept. 13, politically crushed after 2 months in office. He died in Porto Alegre Sept. 26 of cerebral hemorrhage.

Plebiscite Forced by Leftist Strikes

Congress Sept. 14-15 finally scheduled a plebiscite after the leftist General Workers' Command (CGT) had launched nationwide work stoppages Sept. 14 in support of the plebiscite demand. The strikers also demanded (a) an 80%-to-100% raise in minimum wages, (b) a "radical agrarian reform" program and (c) a freeze on the prices of essential consumer goods.

The walkouts tied up railroad and maritime transport in and from the states of Rio de Janeiro, Sao Paulo and Pernambuco. The city of Sao Paulo declared the strike there illegal, and police dispersed pickets who were trying to force the Bank of Sao Paulo State to close. Union leaders were arrested in Sao Paulo and in Rio de Janeiro State.

Gen. Osvino Ferreira Alves, commander of the First Army and a reputed left-wing nationalist, prevented Guanabara State police Sept. 14 from arresting union leaders in the city of Rio de Janeiro. (Gov. Carlos Lacerda of Guanabara was Pres. Goulart's chief political foe.) Alves thereby blocked the arrest of such prominent strike leaders as Benedito Cerqueira, president of the Rio de Janeiro metalworkers' union and a member of the Communist-led World Federation of Trade Unions, and Osvaldo Pacheco of the National Port Workers' Union. (A serious and growing split was beginning to appear in the armed forces over political actions by Alves and other pro-Goulart nationalistic commanders. Gen. Decio Escobar, director of war materiel, apparently spoke for many leading officers when he said Nov. 11 at a Rio de Janeiro ceremony attended by more than 30 generals: "Politics in the army or the army in politics is an evil that must be combatted without truce. Military pressure for political and social reforms is as odious as the pressure from organized labor.")

In Brasilia, the Senate voted 34-19 Sept. 14 to approve the scheduling Jan. 6, 1963 of a countrywide plebiscite on the parliamentary system of government. The Chamber of Deputies concurred Sept. 15 by 169-83 vote. The main opposition came from conservative members of the National Democratic Union (UDN).

When news of Congress' action reached the country's industrial centers Sept. 16, the strikers returned to work.

Lima Heads Cabinet

Pres. Goulart Sept. 17 named ex-Labor Min. Hermes Lima, 59, as premier. Lima assumed the additional post of foreign minister in a caretaker cabinet sworn in Sept. 18.

Lima's cabinet contained 6 members of Brochado's outgoing cabinet, including Finance Min. Miguel Calmon (who replaced Walter Moreira Salles when the latter resigned Sept. 3) and 2 of the 3 military ministers, Adm. Pedro de Araujo Suzano (navy) and Brig. Joaquim Reinaldo de Carvalho (air). Gen. Amaury Kruel, who had been appointed by Goulart as acting war minister after Brochado's cabinet resigned, replaced Nelson de Melo as war minister. Brochado's foreign minister, Afonso Arinois de Melo Franco was named to head Brazil's UN delegation. Ex-War Min. Henrique Teixeira Lott was named mines and energy minister but rejected the appointment, and the post went to Eliezer Batista.

Goulart Sept. 27 signed Decree No. 1422, creating the position of minister extraordinary for planning. He appointed Celso Furtado to the new post with orders to prepare a 3-year plan for national economic development. Furtado, who until then had been director of the Superintendency for Economic Development of the Northeast (SUDENE), also assumed responsibility in his new position for supply and price policies, coordination of the activities of SUDENE with those of the other 3 regional development agencies (for the Southwest frontier area, Amazonia and the Sao Francisco Valley) and, generally, for all programs of foreign aid to Brazil.

(Following the Oct. 7 election, the outgoing Chamber of Deputies returned to session and confirmed Lima as premier Nov. 30 by 164 votes—a bare majority of the 326-seat lower house. The deputies also approved Brazil's draft budget for 1963. The new budget had an estimated deficit of 251 billion cruzeiros, or about $500 million.)

Congressional & Gubernatorial Elections

Brazil's Congressional and state gubernatorial elections took place Oct. 7 and revealed the uneven pattern of political and social development of the nation. 14,747,221 of about 18½ million eligible Brazilian voters went to the polls. The conservative nature of a large part of the electorate was indicated when

(a) Janio Quadros failed to win the governorship of Sao Paulo, and (b) ultranationalist Leonel Brizola's candidate for governor was defeated in Rio Grande do Sul while (c) left-wing candidate Miguel Arraes de Alencar won the governorship of the northeastern state of Pernambuco. Highlighting the 11 gubernatorial elections were 3 important races, and in the Congressional elections there was a highly emotional contest in Guanabara.

In Pernambuco, Miguel Arraes received 264,616 votes as the Brazilian Labor Party (PTB) and left-wing parties' candidate for governor; his opponent, the conservative Joao Cleofas, received 251,707 votes. In Sao Paulo, Quadros' bid to return to politics as governor failed; his old rival Ademar de Barros, also an ex-governor of the state, won by 1,249,414 votes to Quadros' 1,125,941. (A 3d candidate, Jose Bonifacio Coutinho Nogueira, received approximately 722,000 votes.) In Rio Grande do Sul, Leonel Brizola's PTB failed to elect Egydio Michaelsen as governor. The victor was Ildo Meneghetti, who ran on a 5-party coalition (PSD-PL-PDC-UDN-PSP) ticket. Meneghetti received 502,356 votes to Michaelsen's 480,131. Brizola, whose term as governor of Rio Grande do Sul was ended, was quoted in *O Estado de Sao Paulo* Oct. 14 as saying that the Catholic Church had "scandalously protected" opposition candidates and that this had seriously handicapped Labor Party candidates.

Gov. Brizola, running for Congress from the city of Rio de Janeiro in Guanabara State, received more than 258,000 votes, won an overwhelming victory and increased the prestige of PTB's ultranationalist wing.

In the new state of Acre, carved off from Amazonas State's southwestern extremity, Jose Augusto Araujo, PTB candidate, was elected governor. In Amazonas itself, Plinio Coelho, backed by an alliance of the PTB and Christian Democratic Party (PDC), won the gubernatorial election. In Rio de Janeiro, gubernatorial victor Badger Silveira led a PTB-PDC alliance to power.

5 gubernatorial elections took place in Brazil's socially and economically troubled Northeast; Miguel Arraes' victory in Pernambuco was the most notable. Petronio Portela (PSD-UDN) won in Piaui, Seixas Doria (PSD) in Sergipe, Virgilio

Tavora (UDN) in Ceara and Lomanto Junior (UDN-PTB-PR-PL-PRP-PST) in Bahia.

In the Congressional elections, the entire Chamber of Deputies (whose membership was expanded by 78 seats to a total of 409) was chosen, and 45 of Brazil's 66 Senate seats were contested in the 22 states. (Brazil's Electoral Court subsequently annulled the results in contests for 2 Senate seats from Minas Gerais State, where more than half the registered voters had failed to vote.) The Congressional results:

	Deputies	Senators
Social Democratic (PSD)	122	23
Brazilian Labor (PTB)	97	18
National Democratic (UDN)	96	17
Progressive Socialist (PSP)	23	2
Christian Democratic (PDC)	18	0
Republican (PR)	13	0
National Labor (PTN)	10	2
Social Workers' (PST)	6	0
Popular Representation (PRP)	5	0
Labor Reform Movement (MRT)	4	1
Brazilian Socialist (PSB)	4	1
Rural Workers' (PRT)	3	0
Liberation (PL)	3	2

Members of all of Brazil's 22 state assemblies were also chosen in the Oct. 7 elections.

Cuban Missile Crisis

Cuban affairs and the missile confrontation between the U.S. and USSR provoked the first serious political problem for Hermes Lima as premier, and Lima Oct. 23 upheld "Cuba's right to carry out its political experiment." Speaking at a pro-Cuba demonstration outside the Foreign Ministry building in Rio de Janeiro, Lima said: "The fact that a Socialist regime exists in Cuba does not mean that it is not an American regime"; "Latin America is not bound in serfdom to any international interests that oblige us to maintain a type of regime in which the people do not find conditions for their material improvement and national liberation."

Police in Rio de Janeiro Oct. 25 broke up a demonstration of 800 pro-Castro sympathizers attempting to march on the U.S. embassy in protest against the U.S.' blockade of Cuba. Police fired submachine guns and used tear gas, clubs and water hoses in dispersing the demonstrators.

Pres. Goulart sent Gen. Alvino da Silva, chief of the Brazilian presidential military staff, to Havana Oct. 29 as his personal emissary to study the possibility for a negotiated settlement of Cuba's relations with the other Western Hemisphere nations. Da Silva conferred with Castro shortly after Da Silva's arrival and met with UN Acting Secy. Gen. U Thant Oct. 31, but the Brazilian role in the affair appeared to be minimal.

U.S. Relations Under Strain

U.S.-Brazilian relations came under heavy pressure in December from the more radical of Brazilian nationalists. Premier Lima Dec. 4 dismissed Joao Pinheiro as labor minister and named National Labor Director Benjamin Eurico Cruz to succeed him after Pinheiro refused to retract a TV statement in which he had attacked Brazil's ambassador to Washington and a leading federal finance official for their economic-policy views.

Pinheiro had criticized Amb.-to-U.S. Roberto de Oliveira Campos and Dr. Octavio Gouveia Bulhoes, director of Brazil's Superintendency of Currency & Credit (SUMOC), for supporting International Monetary Fund (IMF) proposals on solving the country's inflation. Pinheiro also maintained that Brazil's economic problems could not be solved until Campos and Bulhoes were dismissed. The U.S. was known to favor the IMF's position.

Washington soon gave indications of U.S. pressure on the Goulart administration. Pres. Kennedy at his news conference Dec. 12 took note of Brazil's financial plight and expressed official concern. In a speech Dec. 14 before the Economic Club of New York, Kennedy maintained that the U.S. could not help Brazil while its inflation continued to soar at the annual rate of 50%. U.S. officials also questioned Brazil's stand in the Cuban missile crisis and Goulart's refusal to temper the anti-U.S. positions of his leftist supporters, including Deputy Leonel Brizola, his brother-in-law.

Brazilian officials arranged for a visit by U.S. Atty. Gen. Robert F. Kennedy, the U.S. President's brother, in an attempt to improve relations with the U.S. Kennedy arrived in Brasilia Dec. 17 and conferred with Goulart for 3 hours. Dr. Celso Furtado, minister extraordinary for planning, presented to

Kennedy a 15-page summary of a 3-year plan he had drafted for Brazilian economic development. Kennedy then returned to the U.S. Dec. 18.

Goulart came under fire from Brazilian ultranationalists immediately for having met with Kennedy. Goulart denied that he and Robert Kennedy, as Pres. Kennedy's agent, had reached any secret agreement. He claimed in an interview reported Dec. 19 in the conservative morning daily *Jornal do Brasil* (of Rio de Janeiro) that his meeting with the U.S. attorney general had "dissipate[d] all negative impressions" held by the U.S. government about Brazil and its political leadership. Goulart said he and Kennedy had discussed: (a) Brazil's balance of payments problems (created by falling prices of its traditional exports and rising prices of industrial equipment and imports); (b) the Alliance for Progress; (c) the Cuban crisis and the Latin American situation in general.

3-Year Economic Plan

The 1963-5 economic development program aimed at maintaining Brazil's industrial growth and checking its inflation was made public by the government Dec. 30 after much speculative comment in Brazil's press.

The plan, approved by the cabinet, called for a 7% annual increase in the gross national product. This was to be achieved through the investment of about $7 billion, largely in the industrial field. Among the plan's measures aimed at curbing inflation: (a) a reduction in public expenditures in the 1963 budget; (b) the floating of treasury notes to finance work not covered by revenues.

A favorable trade balance of about $700 million was foreseen for the 1963-5 period. But the economy planners felt that the government would be required to seek $1½ billion in foreign loans and debt postponement during the period.

The plan had been devised by Dr. Furtado, who envisaged limitations on salary increases and on credit. Furtado also proposed price ceilings, the cancellation of certain government subsidies and further devaluation of the cruzeiro.

Other major proposals of the plan:

Education—The government should make provision for 6 years of education for children in urban areas and for 4 years of education for children in rural areas.

Electric power—333 billion cruzeiros and $180 million in foreign exchange would be invested toward increasing power capacity from 4.7 million kilowatts to 7.4 million kilowatts.

Telecommunications—The government should spend 45 billion cruzeiros to expand and modernize telegraph, postal and radio services.

Petroleum—Brazil's state oil monopoly, Petrobras, should set a target of 42.2 million barrels of oil to be produced in 1965. The government should invest 230 billion cruzeiros in Brazil's petroleum and petrochemical industries to achieve this aim.

World Coffee Agreement

The International Coffee Agreement, setting quotas for 36 coffee-exporting countries for 5 years, had been approved at a UN coffee conference Aug. 25 and signed by Sept. 28 by Brazil and 22 other governments. Brazil received the largest annual quota, 18 million standard 132-pound bags, 600,000 more than Brazil's current annual level and about ⅖ of the total world output.

1963

POLITICAL & ECONOMIC WOES

1963 was a crucial year for the Goulart administration. Inflation rose by 80.7% while the gross domestic product's growth rate fell by 3.8 points to a mere 1.6%. Increasing public tension sustained by a mounting wave of strikes by labor unions (for both political and economic ends) and barely contained social unrest, drained Pres. Joao Goulart's prestige. An uprising of noncommissioned officers in September, quickly put down, was capped by Congress' refusal in October to grant Goulart state-of-siege powers he had requested for a 30-day span in which to rule unchecked.

Politically, 1963 was a time of partisan realignments, a bid by the lower military for direct political representation and, finally, the beginnings of a bitter showdown between forces led by Goulart and those of his political enemies. The anti-Goulart groups marshalled themselves behind Guanabara Gov. Carlos Lacerda, supported by Govs. Ademar de Barros of Sao Paulo State, Jose Magalhaes Pinto of Minas Gerais State and much of the top-ranking military. The year began with a plebiscite overwhelmingly indorsing a return to the presidential system of government. Its climax was a fatal blaze of gunfire on the floor of the federal Senate. It ended unusually, with the Congress still in session over the Christmas holidays to guard against the chance that Goulart would unilaterally decree a state of siege.

141

Presidential Government Restored

At least 11 million of Brazil's 18½ million eligible voters cast ballots Jan. 6 in a plebiscite that resulted in the abandonment of the 16-month-old parliamentary system of government and Brazil's return to a strong presidential form of administration. The parliamentary system was rejected by a vote of about 8 to 1, although no final, accurate figures were made public. Congress accepted the results of the plebiscite. The Senate voted 42-0 Jan. 18 and the Chamber of Deputies 258-9 Jan. 22 to put into effect the popular decision to reinstate the strong executive form of government.

The cabinet of Premier Hermes Lima resigned Jan. 22. Goulart, retaining Lima as his foreign affairs minister, announced the makeup of a new cabinet Jan. 24.

The Jan. 24 cabinet: Finance—Francisco San Tiago Dantas. Transportation & Public Works—Helio Almeida. Industry & Commerce—Antonio Balbino. Labor—Almino Afonso. Education & Culture—Teotonio Monteiro de Barros. Mines & Energy—Eliezer Batista. Agriculture—Jose Ermiro de Moraes. War—Maj. Gen. Amaury Kruel. Navy—Adm. Pedro Paulo de Araujo Suzano. Air—Brig. Joaquim Reinaldo de Carvalho, Justice—Joao Mangabeira, Health—Paulo Pinheiro Chagas, Special minister for administrative reform— Ernani do Amaral Peixoto. Dr. Celso Furtado continued as minister extraordinary for planning.

Agrarian Reform Program Rejected

Pres. Goulart Mar. 22 sent to Congress an agrarian reform bill that included proposals for the expropriation of unused private land and the distribution of this land among rural and other workers in the region involved. But the measure was killed in committee in mid-May.

The bill proposed that compensation for expropriated land should be in the form of 6%, 20-year public-debt bonds of adjustable value rather than cash payment in advance as prescribed by Article 141 of the 1946 constitution. If land were expropriated for the "social interest"—a motive made valid in the constitution—the bill would give the owner the privilege of choosing adjacent land equal in size to his former holding.

The bill also provided that minimum proportions of each type of property would be assigned to producing food for the domestic market. The bill was prepared at the direction of Planning Min. Celso Furtado as a supplement to his 3-year economic development plan.

160 conservative members of the federal Chamber of Deputies supported an alternative bill introduced Apr. 24 by UDN Deputy Herbert Levy. They also signed a manifesto that scored the administration proposal's provision permitting expropriations in the "social interest." They pointed out that the federal and state governments already held title to 2/3 of the land surface of Brazil. They also argued that the proposal's provision for compensation in state bonds rather than in cash, as stipulated in the 1946 constitution, represented a "suppression of fundamental rights" and stamped the measure as "demagogic."

Congressional action on the bill came to a halt in mid-May when a special committee of the Chamber of Deputies rejected the measure by 7-4 vote. Those voting in favor of the program were Arraudo Sampaio of the Christian Democrats and Leonel Brizola, Bocaiuva Cunha and Doutel de Andrada of the Brazilian Labor Party.

Goulart fruitlessly took his case for agrarian reform to the people after the Chamber of Deputies bottled up his proposal in committee. The president went to Sao Paulo May 26 to enlist labor support for the reform and spoke in its behalf that weekend. He spoke at the law school. He also visited high church officials in an effort to mobilize church support.

Drought & Fire Menace Coffee Crop

A severe drought parched the soil of Parana, Brazil's leading coffee-growing state, during 1963. The dry period began late in January and continued for 7 months, creating a highly dangerous condition in the southeastern state's pine forests.

Fires in late summer caused about 250 deaths and injured 500 persons. The blazes swept through the forests and across the plantations. 300,000 people fled before the conflagration. The U.S. sent blood plasma and food for the survivers.

Parties Realigned, Goulart Under Attack

Political fragmentation had virtually disappeared in the newly elected Brazilian Congress when it convened in February after Deputy Sergio Magalhaes, a Brazilian Laborite from Guanabara State, had succeeded in temporarily grouping left-wing nationalist deputies into a bloc called the *Frente Parlamentar Nacionalista* (FPN, or Nationalist Parliamentary Front). Supporting the FPN was the General Workers Command (CGT), which warned Apr. 12 that there would be a general strike if right-wing elements attempted a coup. The National Students Union (UNE) also supported the FPN.

Conservative Deputy Joao Mendes, a National Democrat from Bahia, countered by forming the *Acao Democratica Parlamentar* (ADP, or Democratic Parliamentary Action), a group stressing Pan Americanism and the superior merits of private enterprise.

Brazil's former political alliances gave way, and the left-wing and right-wing forces in Congress ranged themselves directly against each other. Pres. Goulart's Brazilian Labor Party (PTB) supported the FPN, and the National Democratic Union (UDN) gave its support to the ADP.

Goulart came under heavy political fire in April from left- and right-wing elements. Both attacked the president for his supporting of Planning Min. Furtado's 3-year economic plan. The left-wing called it a sell-out to the demands of the International Monetary Fund and warned that it would harm the lower income groups. *O Estado de Sao Paulo,* mirroring conservative views, editorialized that the plan was "unrealistic" and did not pay enough attention to the problems of agriculture and foreign capital. Deputy Munhoz da Rocha, a Sao Paulo conservative, called the plan "inflationary." Both sides considered the project a blueprint for disaster for Brazil's future development. Conservative Congressmen were also extremely critical of Goulart's land-reform bill. The National Democratic Union's leading spokesman, Gov. Carlos Lacerda of Guanabara, meanwhile, denounced Goulart for promoting "dictatorship in Brazil" and dismissed the land-reform bill as a hoax.

Brazilian Laborite Deputy Leonel Brizola of Guanabara, ex-governor of Rio Grande do Sul, led the left-wing nationalist Congressmen's attack on Goulart, his brother-in-law. Brizola criticized the administration for alleged concessions to conservatism and for bowing to the International Monetary Fund's austerity demands.

Brizola called Apr. 6 for radical leftists to rally in Rio de Janeiro. Gen. Osvino Ferreira Alves, commander of the First Army (stationed in Rio de Janeiro), promptly indorsed Brizola's summons. A brief military feud flared as War Min. Amaury Kruel rebuked the general for playing politics. The rally was finally cancelled Apr. 8 on Goulart's request.

Brizola maintained pressure on the Goulart administration by attacking the policies of Finance Min. Francisco San Tiago Dantas, and he also criticized conservative military officials. Brizola indorsed the outcome of a May 11 rally of more than 1,000 noncommissioned officers in Rio de Janeiro. At the rally, army Warrant Officer Gelci Rodrigues Correa had urged a concerted effort on behalf of direct political representation for their ranks. Correa advocated that his colleagues take up arms if necessary against the "forces of reaction" in order to obtain desired constitutional reforms. (War Min. Kruel May 12 ordered 15 to 30 days of detention for Correa and 7 other noncommissioned officers who had attended the rally. Kruel demanded better army discipline.) In August, Brizola called for greater action on the part of the *Frente de Mobilizacao Popular* (FMP, or Popular Mobilization Front), which had been organized outside Congress to coordinate the activities of various political groups favoring nationalist and radical political reforms.

Cabinet Reorganized

Goulart drastically revised his cabinet in mid-June in an effort to win wider political support for his government's fiscal reform and economic policies. With the appointment of Prof. Carlos de Carvalho Pinto, ex-governor of Sao Paulo State, as his new finance minister, Goulart introduced the Christian Democratic Party—with which Carvalho Pinto, nominally of the National Democratic Union, was closely allied—into closer communication with his administration. Goulart retained Ernani Peixoto as special minister for administrative reforms.

The other cabinet members named: Evandro Lins e Silva, foreign affairs; Abelardo Araujo Jurema, justice and interior; Egydio Michaelsen, industry and commerce; Antonio Ferreira de Oliveira Brito, mines and energy; Espedito Machado Ponte, transport and public works; Osvaldo Cavalcanti Costa Lima Filho, agriculture; Amaury de Oliveira e Silva, labor and social security; Paulo de Tarso Santos, education and culture; Dr. Wilson Fadul, health; Gen. Jair Dantas Ribeiro, war; Adm. Sylvio Borges de Souza Motta, navy; Brig. Anisio Botelho, air.

Goulart appointed outgoing Finance Min. Francisco San Tiago Dantas to lead an economic mission to the U.S. and to western and eastern Europe. Celso Furtado ceased to be minister extraordinary for planning, but Goulart did not name a replacement. (Furtado became director of SUDENE in September.) Deputy Tancredo Neves, a Social Democrat and ex-premier, became government leader in the Chamber of Deputies.

Joao Augusto de Araujo Castro, 44, a career officer in the Brazilian foreign service, succeeded Evandro Lins e Silva as foreign minister Aug. 22 after Lins e Silva was appointed to the Brazilian Supreme Court. (Castro had helped draft ex-Pres. Juscelino Kubitschek's Operation Pan America proposal of June 1958.) Goulart also named Gen. Argemiro Assis Brasil to succeed Col. Joao Sarmento as head of the president's military household, a cabinet-rank post designed to keep the president informed of the opinions of top-ranking military, naval and air officers.

In a message to the country, Goulart had outlined the new government's duties June 22 as protecting workers' purchasing power, assuring peaceful conditions for free enterprise, accelerating effective federal administration, improving living standards, braking inflation, widening employment and increasing production.

Goulart, campaigning for his agrarian reform proposals, promised to lead a leftist rally in Rio de Janeiro to be held in honor of the late Getulio Vargas Aug. 23. Heavy military cover was ordered for the meeting, and Gov. Carlos Lacerda of Guanabara listed Aug. 23 and 24 as public holidays in his state in order to avoid clashes between his supporters and the president's. At the rally Goulart urged insistently that the Congress pass constitutional amendments necessary to enable the reforms to be enacted and thus to forestall their being carried out "outside the law." Various General Workers' Command (CGT) leaders appeared on the platform with Goulart.

Noncoms' Uprising in Brasilia

More than 600 air force and marine sergeants, corporals and other enlisted men rose in rebellion in Brasilia Sept. 12—and surrendered the same day. They acted one day after Brazil's Supreme Court had held in a 7-1 decision Sept. 11 that noncommissioned officers were ineligible to run for elective public office.

Before surrendering, the rebels seized the central telephone and telegraph offices, the military and civilian airports and the Navy Ministry. They took over the Central Brazil Foundation's radio transmitter and broadcast a futile appeal to other enlisted personnel officers to join them.

The insurgents surrendered their airport strongpoints without resistance. But government troops had to shoot their way into the Navy Ministry building, where they killed one rebel and wounded 3 others. More than 550 rebels were arrested, including their leader, identified as air force First Sgt. Antonio Prestes de Paulo.

The rebels released these hostages they had held during the 10-hour revolt: Chamber of Deputies Pres. Clovis Mota, Supreme Court Justice Victor Nunes Leal and 30 military officers.

A War Ministry communique said the rebellion was a protest against the Sept. 11 Supreme Court decision upholding a lower court's refusal to certify the election of a sergeant (of the federalized state police) to the Rio Grande do Sul State legislature.

Pres. Goulart Sept. 14 publicly supported his cabinet's service ministers, who had ordered a thorough military probe of the uprising. Goulart declared that military discipline breaches would not be tolerated, whatever the justice of any group's demands.

Political tension and suspicion between radical and conservative forces increased after Leonel Brizola appealed Sept. 14 over the Mayrink Veiga radio station in Rio de Janeiro for support for the noncoms. Brizola declared that the Popular Mobilization Front (FMP), the National Students' Union (UNE) and the General Workers' Command (CGT) would defend the right of noncommissioned officers to hold public office.

Ex-Pres. Juscelino Kubitschek held Sept. 14 that there was nothing abnormal about the noncom revolt and added that he supported the sergeants' claim to the right to hold elective public office. Kubitschek, then a Senator from Goias, made these remarks to newsmen in Sao Paulo, where he was starting his 1965 presidential campaign.

Gen. Peri Constant Bevilacqua, commander of the 2d Army (located in Sao Paulo), described the CGT Sept. 18 as "enemies of law, order and democratic institutions." Commanders of the 3d and 4th Army Regions and ex-Pres. Eurico Dutra (1945-50) wired support for Bevilacqua's statement. The CGT responded Sept. 21 with a statement calling for workers to unite with nationalist "officers, sergeants and soldiers" to force a reform of old laws. (Goulart announced Nov. 18 that he had appointed Gen. Amaury Kruel to replace Bevilacqua as commander of the 2d Army. Bevilacqua had received an official warning against making further political statements.)

Many of the enlisted men arrested Sept. 12 were released in November from military custody.

Lacerda 'Kidnap' Fails

An unsuccessful attempt was apparently made Oct. 4 to kidnap or arrest Gov. Carlos Lacerda of Guanabara. Gen. Alfredo Pinheiro, paratroop batallion commander, ordered Lt. Col. Abelardo Mafra and a Lt. Col. Cavalcanti to intercept Lacerda as he was inspecting a new hospital installation in Rio de Janeiro. The 2 officers were delayed in traffic. When they arrived at the hospital, the governor had already left. Nearly 2 months later War Min. Jair Dantas Ribeiro ordered the arrest of Cavalcanti, who had asserted that Pinheiro had ordered him to seize Lacerda.

The alleged kidnap attempt took place at a time when Lacerda was locked in a political power struggle with Pres. Goulart. Lacerda, in virtual political control of Brazil's biggest city, used TV, radio and the press for repeated attacks on Goulart, who felt himself forced to come back often to Rio de Janeiro from Brasilia in order to defend his administration. The labor unions, which considered themselves favored by Goulart, held mass meetings and demonstrations to show support for the president.

Congress Defies Goulart

Pres. Goulart apparently was becoming increasingly unable to exercise decisive control over the country's political affairs. This was illustrated in October, when Congressional opposition to his policies had become very strong and Goulart failed in an effort to persuade Congress to give him state-of-siege powers.

The Goulart administration asked Congress Oct. 4 to declare a state of siege for 30 days during which, it said, it would attempt to cope with a "serious internal commotion" that was threatening "democratic institutions and political order." In asking for state-of-siege powers, Justice Min. Abelardo Jurema implied that Govs. Carlos Lacerda of Guanabara and Ademar de Barros of Sao Paulo were involved with Goulart's opponents in a "conspiracy to seize power by overthrowing the regime."

Goulart had been pressured by the armed forces to seek emergency powers to combat what they cited as a threat posed by inflation, subversion, strikes and the enlisted men's abortive revolt. A statement by the military leaders said: " ... It is indispensable ... to resort to a state of siege ... to avoid internal commotion which might break out at any time in the country."

Goulart also was reported to be seeking the ouster of Lacerda, who had criticized the government's policies as inflationary and had charged Communist infiltration of the Goulart regime. The armed forces chiefs had accused Lacerda and de Barros of agitating against the Goulart government. A railroad walkout had been called Oct. 3 in de Barros' state, Sao Paulo.

In opposing the proposed state of siege, the National Democratic Union (2d largest party in Congress) declared Oct. 5 that there was "no serious internal disorder in the country nor any evidence that any was likely to break out." The party said the government's purpose actually was aimed at suspending fundamental rights and "increasing military jurisdiction over the citizens." Opposition to the proposed state of siege also had been expressed by members of the centrist Social Democratic Party, by extreme leftists in Goulart's Brazilian Labor Party and by the National Parliamentary Front, composed of leftists and nationalists of all parties.

O Estado of Sao Paulo reported Oct. 19 that Gen. Humberto Castelo Branco, chief of the Joint Military Staff Command (*chefe do Estado Maior do Exercito*), had written to War Min. Jair Dantas Ribeiro a letter indicating that many high-ranking officers felt the support given by Ribeiro to Goulart's request for state-of-seige powers was ill-advised and not in accord with the general wishes of the highest-ranking military officials. *O Estado* asserted that Castelo Branco's letter was significant in view of "insistent rumors" that Castelo Branco had been invited to be war minister.

Goulart withdrew the state-of-seige request Oct. 7 in the face of the the overwhelming opposition. Goulart said in a message to Congress that "the government no longer needs the concession of extraordinary measures for the task of maintaining republican institutions." An accompanying statement from the 3 armed forces ministers, led by Ribeiro, said Goulart was "permanently devoted to the defense of the real interests of the country" and "preoccupied with the direction of political events that could create a favorable climate for the destruction of the regime."

Goulart's Brazilian Labor Party (PTB) had become the dominant party in the Chamber of Deputies of the National Congress in November. This came about when 7 deputies shifted their allegiance from the Social Democratic Party (PSD), the erstwhile dominant party. The shifts altered the respective voting strengths of the 3 leading parties in the lower house. Party strengths following the changes: PTB, 121 deputies; PSD, 117; National Democratic Union, 95.

Congress adopted an extraordinary course of action Dec. 16 by deciding to remain in session over the Christmas holidays lest Goulart take advantage of its absence to declare a state of siege.

Education & Culture Min. Paulo de Tarso had resigned in mid-October in protest against what he was said to regard as a political "opening toward the center" on Goulart's part.

Prof. Carlos de Carvalho Pinto resigned Dec. 19 as finance minister. Goulart Dec. 20 appointed Ney Neves Galvao to succeed him. Labor interests and left-wing nationalists hailed Galvao's appointment, but many critics held that the choice was unwise. They charged that Galvao was too weak to formulate and adhere to sound fiscal policy and that the power of Galvao's office, therefore, would be exercised by Goulart, who, they complained, placed the satisfaction of social wants ahead of solvency.

Battle Against Inflation

Before being replaced as finance minister, Francisco San Tiago Dantas had undertaken to check the country's worsening inflation.

On Dantas' orders, a measure was drafted to set up a National Monetary Council that would create a flexible federal monetary control system after the style of the U.S. Federal Reserve banks but that would not replace the Bank of Brazil as the government's bank. Another of Dantas' financial measures called for the establishment of a National Rural Credit Committee to set controls over farm credit policy. Goulart sent a bill embodying these proposals to Congress Mar. 23.

At Dantas' urging, Goulart announced Feb. 14 that the government was asking Brazil's industrialists to hold down prices of manufactured goods to then prevailing levels; he said that the government would put a 40% ceiling on forthcoming wage and salary increases for military personnel and federal civil servants.

But Goulart announced Apr. 29 that armed-forces and civil-service pay increments due in April would average 60%. In breaking his promise to hold the raises to 40%, Goulart apparently bent to political pressure. Then, under presumably increasing pressure, Congress passed and Goulart July 17 signed into law a bill that gave pay raises of 70% to civilian, military, naval and air force employes of the federal government, retroactive to June 1. To finance the raises, the law required the contribution of compulsory credits to the National Industrial Investment Fund. These were charged at the rate of from 1.56% to 15% during 1963-5 on all personal incomes above 884,000 cruzeiros. The credits would earn interest at 6% annually and accrue for repayment in 1966 and 1967.

The left-wing General Workers' Command (CGT) late in October called a general strike in the state of Sao Paulo and demanded a 100% wage increase for the majority of unions involved. (The CGT had already called out Sao Paulo's railroad workers for one day Oct. 3.) Goulart indicated that he considered the CGT's demands justifiable. But Gen. Peri Bevilacqua, commander of the 2d Army in Sao Paulo, joined forces with Sao Paulo State police in arresting more than 600 strikers, and he provided protection for those workers wanting to return to their jobs before the end of the strike. The Sao Paulo labor court declared the walkout illegal, and it soon collapsed. The court also ruled, however, that the workers were entitled to an 80% wage increase. (A spokesman for the Usiminas steel mill, a joint Japanese-Brazilian company, reported Oct. 7 that municipal police had fired into demonstrating strikers at the plant in the state of Minas Gerais; 7 workers were killed and 49 injured.)

Goulart, in a message to Congress, proposed Dec. 4 that Brazil pay a bonus equivalent to one month's wages to 250,000 civil service workers. (A law setting up such a bonus for private employes throughout Brazil had taken effect in January.) It was estimated that such a bonus, to apply to state enterprises, such as the railroads (then operating at a deficit), would require outlays of more than 80 billion cruzeiros ($130 million).

Faced with revolt within the cabinet, however, Goulart abandoned the proposal. Carlos de Carvalho Pinto, who had replaced Dantas as finance minister, had reportedly threatened Dec. 6 to resign over the issue.

The Getulio Vargas Foundation estimated that the cost of living for the working class had gone up 80.7% in 1963. The Labor Ministry reported that the cost of living in the city of Rio de Janeiro had risen 95.8% in 1963.

Another Planned Deficit Approved

The federal government Dec. 7 published the adopted budget for 1964. The estimate was based on expected revenues totaling 1.4788 trillion cruzeiros and projected expenditures of 2.1103 trillion cruzeiros. The total expenditures figure was more than double that for 1963 and so were the individual allocations in most categories.

According to the Bank of London & South America's *Fortnightly Review,* estimates of the actual deficit in Brazil's 1963 financial administration of public affairs varied from 320 billion cruzeiros, as calculated by Finance Min. Carlos de Carvalho Pinto, through 395 billion cruzeiros, as calculated by ex-Finance Min. Francisco San Tiago Dantas, to 417 billion cruzeiros, an estimate "indicated by a Brazilian economic journal." Helping account for such an imbalance, the British periodical reported, were a 91.4 billion-cruzeiro reduction in the federal sales tax below the budget estimate and a 139 billion-cruzeiro revenue loss attributed by the Brazilian press to tax evasion.

Other Economic Developments

An International Monetary Fund spokesman had announced in Washington, D.C. June 5 that the IMF had decided not to grant Brazil's request for $100 million in standby credits but would permit Brazil to draw $60 million to meet balance-of-payments deficits caused by a decline in export earnings.

Goulart Oct. 27 proposed keeping a stricter grip on the outflow of foreign profits. In a memo to Finance Min. Carvalho Pinto, Goulart declared that the law then in force should not consider profits reinvested in Brazil by foreign companies as a basis for calculating the legal maximum that such companies could remit abroad as profits. (The law, passed in 1962, provided that a firm based outside Brazil could annually remit in profits from Brazil an amount equal at most to 10% of its registered capital investment in Brazil. It was asserted in some reports that as much as $100 million in accumulated profits was being held back pending remittance authorization by the Superintendency of Currency & Credit.)

Goulart Dec. 23 signed a decree authorizing Brazilian oil refineries to process only crude oil (a) produced in Brazil, (b) imported under inter-government agreements or (c) issued from federal government supplies. This would hamper the operations of foreign-owned oil companies.

Relations with the U.S.

Brazilian Amb.-to-U.S. Roberto Oliveira Campos had returned to Brazil in January for consultations with the Goulart administration on relations between Brazil and the U.S. U.S.-Brazilian relations had cooled as a result of U.S. insistence on austerity in Brazil's economic affairs, curbs on deficits and checks on inflation. At the same time, the U.S. began diplomatic moves for adequate payment for American investments lost when Rio Grande do Sul State expropriated privately owned utilities.

An emergency 90-day $30 million U.S. loan to Brazil, however, had been announced by the U.S. State Department Jan. 7. The funds, made available from the U.S. Treasury, were to be used to enable Brazil to continue some imports on short-term credit despite the huge deficit in its balance of international payments and its virtually complete lack of foreign exchange. The loan represented a partial change in the U.S.' fiscal policy toward Brazil. U.S. loans approved for Brazil in May 1961 had not been disbursed since 1962 because of Washington's feeling that Brazil had not done enough to solve its inflationary problems or to counter anti-U.S. actions by prominent Brazilian officials.

Brazil's role in the Cuban missile crisis—one of strict neutrality plus hints that Brazil was willing to make available its good offices as an impartial mediator—clashed with the U.S. public's mood of alarm. U.S. Congressional hearings on Latin America showed that this view had official proponents.

Assistant State Secy. (for inter-American affairs) Edwin M. Martin appeared Mar. 11 with Assistant State Secy. (for administration) William J. Crockett and Executive Director, Melbourne L. Spector of the Bureau of Inter-American Affairs as a witness before a subcommittee of the House Appropriations Committee looking into the bureau's request for more than $16 million in budget funds for fiscal 1964. (A 15% salary adjustment for the bureau's employes in Brazil was needed to balance locally prevailing wage levels. The bureau also wanted to set up commercial representation in Belo Horizonte, Curitiba, Porto Alegre and Recife and to increase its commercial staff in Sao Paulo in order to encourage an increase in U.S. exports. The bureau likewise wanted to provide rest-and-recuperation travel funds for its employes and their dependents in Belem. It also had staffs to maintain in Brasilia, Salvador [Bahia State] and Santos.)

Martin told subcommittee Chairman John J. Rooney (D., N.Y.) that Pres. Kennedy was "just about to announce that there will be [established] an Office of Brazilian Affairs." In the new office, Martin said, "one man will head up a staff which does both Agency for International Development and State Department work with respect to Brazil." In response to a question from Rep. Rooney, Martin said: Most Latin American countries were cooperating in the Alliance for Progress' effort to have its 20 member countries set up improved tax laws. "Brazil in Dec. [1962] passed a tax law they believe will raise about $225 million additional which is badly needed to try to balance their budget." Brazilian landowners, however, often were able to "avoid paying much of any tax." While the bureau had 162 employes in Brazil, 86 of them Americans, the duties of carrying out consular, visa and special functions left no time "to do a long-range political analysis of [the processes of change characterizing] a country with 80 million covering an area about 1/3 of Latin America...." "We have, I might say, set up a long-range analysis team for Brazil."

Rooney, armed with excerpts from a frank interview granted the *Washington Evening Star* Mar. 11 by Brazilian Finance Min. Francisco San Tiago Dantas, asked Martin Mar. 12 whether it was true that "part of the financial help [Dantas] is seeking from us would be used to develop trade with all countries, including Russia?" Martin said: "It would be unacceptable to have aid provided by us used in any direct fashion to promote trade with the Soviet bloc." "If we recommend aid, it will be for certain specific purposes, and if those purposes are not complied with, then the aid is withdrawn. I think we can tie it up in such a way."

Rooney won from Martin an admission that among documents carried by Dr. Raul Cepero Bonilla (president of the National Bank of Cuba) when he was killed in a Varig (Brazilian airline) jetliner crash in Peru Nov. 27, 1962 had been found several highly controversial letters, copies of which were sent by Peruvian authorities to the Brazilian government.

Martin said: The letters were "correspondence between persons in Brazil and persons in Cuba with respect, primarily, to training for the Peasant Leagues in the Northeast [of Brazil] to take over lands." The letters "are primarily a record of complaints against inefficiency and corruption in the Communist and Cuban apparatus in handling funds made available from Cuba and in recruiting personnel for this operation." "Insofar as these documents are concerned, they indicate very small numbers of people were involved and a very inefficient operation, and yet they do indicate Cuban interest in promotion and financing of what was intended to be guerrilla training" in Brazil.

Rooney asked whether it was true that Brazilian Foreign Min. Hermes Lima "in 1935 ... was expelled from the University of Brazil for his conspiratorial activities during the Communist operations in Brazil that year" and arrested along with the future Justice Min. Joao Mangebeira and another "gentlemen of the Goulart entourage" called simply Ryff. "Isn't it fact," Rooney asked, "that last October [1962], on the day after Pres. Kennedy informed the world about the Russian missions in Cuba, that [the then Premier] Lima told a group of Brazilian 'Castro-Communists' who visited him to express their solidarity with the Castro regime [to the effect] that '... what should be defended in Cuba is that government's right to carry out its present ... [policies because] that government is derived from the self-determination of its people'?"

Martin replied that "something like this [statement] was made about the [same] time [as] Brazil voted with us for the Organization of American States' action with respect to the missiles."

Rooney asked whether Planning Min. Celso Furtado had attended the "founding of the Cominform in 1947," whether Finance Min. Francisco San Tiago Dantas, as foreign minister, had "proposed and defended a coexistence policy with the Communist-Castro regime" while attending a foreign ministers' meeting in Uruguay in Jan. 1962, whether Agriculture Min. Jose Ermiro de Moraes (Rooney called him "Arraes") had "financed the political campaign of [Miguel] Arraes [de Alencar], a Communist who was mayor of Recife and who is now governor of Pernambuco?" Martin suggested that the chairman could be on unsafe ground in calling Gov. Arraes a Communist. "Is [Almino] Afonso..., the minister of labor, properly described as a well-known Communist?" Rooney asked. "No, sir, I don't think so," Martin replied. Rooney asked about reports of purges in the Brazilian armed forces of some officers who had taken "anti-Castro" stands. Martin replied: "There were one or 2 cases of transfers. I recall one in the navy of an officer [Vice Adm. Helio Garnier Sampaio, commander-in-chief of the Brazilian fleet] who publicly recommended that [2 destroyers] be made available for the quarantine [of Cuban ports in the autumn of 1962]. It was considered [that] it was a matter of political importance and policy and not to be advocated by a naval officer until there had been a governmental decision."

"No, sir, I don't think so," Martin replied. Rooney asked about reports of purges in the Brazilian armed forces of some officers who had taken "anti-Castro" stands. Martin replied: "There were one or 2 cases of transfers. I recall one in the navy of an officer [Vice Adm. Helio Garnier Sampeio, commander-in-chief of the Brazilian fleet] who publicly recommended that [2 destroyers] be made available for the quarantine [of Cuban ports in the autumn of 1962]. It was considered [that] it was a matter of political importance and policy and not to be advocated by a naval officer until there had been a governmental decision."

"How about Adm. [Silvio] Heck [the former navy minister] who was arrested after he made public statements concerning the Communist threat to Brazil?" Rooney asked. "I believe this was somewhat earlier," Martin replied. "This, again, was technically based on military interference in political matters." "How about Gen. Emilio Maurel e Filho?" Rooney asked. Martin said he knew nothing about him.

"Are you familiar with Capt. Julio Bierrenbach?" Rooney asked. Martin said he was not. Rooney said: "It is alleged that [Capt. Bierrenbach] was relieved of duty for having returned his Order of Merit naval decoration in protest for decorations awarded to such known Communists as Ryff and [Federal Deputy] Brizola by the department of the navy, and 20 naval officers, including 7 admirals, who sympathized with Capt. Bierrenbach were held under house arrest for 10 days because of their action ... just this past December." Martin replied: "It is my understanding that it proved impossible to find anyone to carry out this order [to put the naval officers under house arrest], and they were not put under detention."

"Do you know whether or not it is the fact that the following Brazilian army officers tried to go to Havana for the 26th-of-July celebration just last year aboard a Cuban plane that had arrived in Rio with Communist propaganda: Gens. Leite, Mendes, Malo, Hunter and Col. Bayar and Maj. Bessara?" Rooney asked. Martin said he was "not familiar with the names in that instance."

Rooney asked whether "Castro-Communist leaders throughout the Western Hemisphere are preparing to meet in Brazil to map strategy for the 2d phase in their campaign to take over Latin America?" "There have been plans for a Cuban solidarity conference Mar. 28 in Rio," Martin acknowledged. "I do not know whether they were going to do at it what you described, but that is not impossible. The Brazilian government has indicated that it did not look with favor on this conference and that it had instructed its consulates abroad not to grant visas for attending it. In fact, there was an article to this effect in this morning's paper, but we have known this for some time."

"Among those making arrangements for this meeting this month in Rio to be called the Continental Congress of Solidarity with Cuba, are certain generals of the Brazilian army involved?" Rooney asked. "There is at least one general," Martin said, "but I am not sure offhand whether he is on the active or retired list: Gen. Luiz Gonzaga Leite, I believe, whom you mentioned earlier." ·

Rooney asked: "... How about Gen. Prestes?—Gen. Cordere Daste?—Gen. Brizola?—You should recognize his name.—Gen. Mastes? On Jan. 31, 1963, in the U[nited] P[ress] I[nternational] dispatch from Rio, it is alleged that on Jan. 31, 1963, in a nationwide television program, Gov. Carlos Lacerda of—Guanabara State ... accuses the government of Brazil of handing over the country to Russia with the aid of U.S. dollars. Are you familiar with that?—What are the facts in that regard?" "Yes, sir," answered Martin. "I think they are quite incorrect."

Rooney's final questions had to do with Brazil's indebtedness to the U.S. and other foreign creditors. After giving it as his own estimate that Brazil would have to pay off in "the next 3 years ... about $1.5 billion to U.S. and European creditors ... about ⅔ of that to U.S. creditors," Martin produced the following table of U.S. aid to Brazil covering the period from July 1, 1946 to June 30, 1962 (all figures in millions of U.S. dollars):

Economic aid:
 AID (and predecessor agencies) assistance:

Development loans	$ 74.7
Development grants	60.9
Other	2.4
Total	138.0
Other economic assistance:	
Public Law 480:	
Loans	203.7
Grants	124.7
Total	328.4
Export-Import Bank (medium and long-term) loans	1,177.0
Inter-American Development Bank (Social Progress Trust Fund)	47.0
Other economic programs	46.4
Total	1,598.8
Total economic aid:	
Loans	1,595.8
Grants	141.0
Total	1,736.8
Military aid	215.9
Total assistance	$1,952.7

Rooney Mar. 15 released testimony made before his subcommittee by U.S. Amb.-to-Brazil Lincoln Gordon on the current political situation in Brazil. Officers of Goulart's Labor Party and other leftists demanded Gordon's ouster following a statement attributed to him that the Brazilian government and the party were infiltrated by Communists. A possible crisis in U.S.-Brazilian relations was averted when the State Department Mar. 20 sent Goulart a note denying that the U.S. government believed that Communists exercised "substantial influence" in Brazil's government. Gordon was reported to have made the charges in his testimony before the subcommittee. The State Department was quick to point out, however, that the department, and not Gordon, was responsible for the allegation. But the department made it clear that Gordon subscribed to the department's views.

The State Department statement, disclosed Mar. 17, said: Brazil's Communist Party membership, "ranging between 25,000 and 40,000," "is small. But their influence is much larger than those small numbers would suggest. The principal field of infiltration and influence is in the labor unions. In the government itself there has been infiltration. The student union is another major area of penetration with the National Student Union now being dominated by Communists."

U.S. State Undersecy. George Ball was reported to have told Brazilian Amb. Roberto Campos in Washington Mar. 18 that the timing of the release of the House testimony was a coincidence and was not intended to undermine current negotiations in Washington between U.S. officials and Brazilian Finance Min. Dantas, who was seeking U.S. financial aid.

An agreement to provide Brazil with $385½ million in U.S. economic aid was concluded following a meeting in Washington Mar. 25 of Dantas and Pres. Kennedy. The meeting climaxed 2 weeks of economic negotiations by Dantas and U.S. officials. The aid was conditional on Brazil's promise to take further measures to combat its economic problems. The agreement, detailed in an exchange of letters between Dantas and David Bell, administrator of the Agency for International Development (AID), provided for:

● $84 million in immediate loans from the Export-Import Bank, the U.S. Treasury and the AID. The loans were designed to prevent the depletion of Brazil's hard currency, resulting largely from the demand for repayment of Brazil's foreign debt, totaling $2.7 billion.

● $200 million in AID loans, ½ of which would be for specific development projects.

● A 7-year extension of a $44½ million Export-Import Bank debt, currently due between June 1 and May 31, 1964.

● $70 million worth of U.S. surplus wheat, repayable in Brazilian cruzeiros.

Dantas, in his letter to Bell, had listed a dozen measures Brazil had taken to bolster its economy. They included tax reform, elimination of the government's special import subsidies on wheat and fuel, rate increases for government railroads and shipping industries and other measures to reduce government spending and the budget deficit and tighten credit and check inflation. In listing other "self-help" economic measures Brazil was taking, Dantas cited current negotiations with the International Monetary Fund and Brazilian pleas for financial aid from the World Bank, private lenders and other governments.

Bell said the U.S. had "been deeply impressed by the way in which this problem has been initiated and by the opportunities it appears to present for constructive international cooperation...."

The Bank of Brazil had announced on the Brazilian government's behalf just after mid-February that it would pay to the International Telephone & Telegraph Co. (IT&T) $7.3 million—half in U.S. dollars and half in cruzeiros—for IT&T's subsidiary, Companhia Telefonica Nacional, taken over by Rio Grande do Sul State in Feb. 1962. IT&T at once announced that a "satisfactory interim arrangement" had been reached with the Brazilian government over the expropriated utility. This statement drew the immediate fire of left-wing nationalists. Goulart promptly held a press conference, at which he claimed that "no payment whatsoever has been made to IT&T as indemnification for its telephone subsidiary expropriated in Porto Alegre."

Brazil settled next with the American & Foreign Power Co. (AFPC), which announced Apr. 22 that it had reached an understanding with the Brazilian government. A Brazilian government agency would buy AFPC's subsidiaries in Brazil for $135 million, pay another $7.7 million as compensation for their uncollected debts and unremitted profits and repay $45.4 million more to cover loans granted by the Export-Import Bank and *Banco Nacional do Desenvolvimento Economico.* As 75% of this compensation would be reinvested in Brazil, the AFPC would receive in transferable currency a total of $33½ million—$10 million on signing the agreement and the balance over 25 years at 6% interest. Brazil would repay the reinvested part remaining of $101½ million in cruzeiros over 25 years at 6½% interest.

Although Brazil's relations with the U.S. had cooled noticeably, Brazilians were profoundly affected by the murder of Pres. John F. Kennedy Nov. 22. Goulart's relations with Kennedy had at times been difficult, and Kennedy's failure to visit Brazil gave rise to comment. The form of his last considerable communication, a personal letter delivered by Amb. tained U.S. State Undersecy. Averell Harriman Nov. 18 in Brasilia, said he was greatly shocked by Kennedy's assassination. Later wrote to Pres. Lyndon B. Johnson of Brazil's grief. The letter, dated Dec. 13, read in part:

... The cruel attack which struck down your predecessor left him, for all time, fixed in the very act of struggling for generous causes and deepened the commitment of all peoples and all men of good will for the construction of a new world, free from the already obsolete ideological preconceptions of the last century and also independent of the unacceptable privileges and interests of special groups, castes or individuals. The causes of improving relations among peoples and of perfecting human society have been fortified by the lamentable episode in which Pres. Kennedy lost his life, Pres. Kennedy who infused both these missions with a higher ideal of justice, with high standards of peaceful brotherhood, and with the search for a prosperity which could be enjoyed by all, in accordance with their merits and their needs....

We are certain, Mr. President, that the policies which were the aspirations of the extraordinarily statesmanlike vision of your lamented predecessor will continue to be pursued with unshakable stubbornness and confidence, within the framework of the strictest respect for human dignity. It is on this postulate that we base the conviction that we are on the right road. No economic process, however perfected, no modern technique, however efficient, will be able to prove lasting and valid if by chance it implies a sacrifice of the dignity of the human individual....

I take pleasure in affirming to you, on this occasion, that this is also the orientation of [the] government of my country. I recognize that, if it lacks this sense of authenticity, no power emanating from the people can expect to be sustained without failing in its mission and its purposes....

Johnson responded in a letter, dated Dec. 18, in which he expressed great appreciation of Goulart's message of sympathy. Johnson also reaffirmed the U.S. government's continuing conviction that "the Alliance for Progress can be of essential importance." Johnson said:

Problems of trade, development and investment ... naturally are of concern to both of us. I believe that all these problems are soluble if approached within a framework of expanding international cooperation—a framework which removes unnecessary barriers to trade and investment and which creates new opportunities for economic growth. This is, of course, especially important to the accelerated growth of the less developed countries....

In the case of Brazil, it appears that there is an immediate concern with the problem of debt payments. Since the U.S. government holds only a relatively small portion of the obligations which are presently due or will fall due in the next few years, a Brazilian initiative to bring this problem within manageable proportions will need to be directed primarily toward arrangements with the commercial creditors, international agencies and governments which account for the bulk of such obligations. The United States, however, stands ready to participate in negotiations for this purpose.

Brazil, I know, is the possessor of a fine tradition of political freedom and stability, and of social and religious tolerance.... The remarkable progress made in the last 30 years, with the creation in Brazil of the greatest industrial center in Latin America, provides solid ground for confidence that all the elements exist for an even more brilliant early future. Our countries have stood together in war and in peace, and I believe that our continued cooperation can make a vital contribution to the welfare of both our peoples.

The text of Johnson's letter was released to the U.S. public Dec. 23. The *N.Y. Times* reported that the letter contained an offer to Goulart of U.S. aid in solving Brazil's debt problem.

Khrushchev Interview

The Soviet mission to the UN Mar. 29 released the text of answers given by Soviet Premier Nikita S. Khrushchev to a number of questions submitted by Paulo Silveira, editor of the afternoon daily *Ultima Hora,* a newspaper in Rio de Janeiro. The timing of the release seemed to indicate an attempt at countering the impact of the recent grant of a \$398½ million financial aid package by the U.S. to Brazil.

In answer to Silveira's first question—*What, in your opinion, are the direct and indirect results of the reestablishment of diplomatic relations between Brazil and the Soviet Union?*—Khrushchev said:

... Between our countries there are no questions at issue that could hamper the development of friendly relations between them. We are convinced that Brazil and the Soviet Union can be good friends and that such friendship would make a great contribution to the cause of promoting international cooperation and preserving world peace. In our opinion it is in that that the positive significance of the restoration of diplomatic relations between our 2 countries lies in the first place....

Since we restored relations, a little more than a year ago, the exchange of trade between our countries has increased more than 50% as compared with 1961.... We are ready to facilitate an increase in the volume of mutual trade
....

We were satisfied by the interest displayed by Brazilians towards the Soviet trade-and-industry exhibition in Rio de Janeiro. Our people enthusiastically acclaimed the performances of talented Brazilian artists in the Soviet Union, where the rich original culture of the Brazilian people is highly appreciated. The resumption of diplomatic relations ... has thus opened broad scope for friendly cooperation between our countries....

Silveira asked—*Besides reciprocal trade, does the USSR regard a policy of active economic cooperation with Brazil*

*with the aim of stepping up the process of our country's
economic development as possible?* Khrushchev affirmed this
emphatically:

While assisting other countries in the development of their economy, we do
not attach any political or other strings infringing the sovereignty of the
country but build our mutual relations on equality and mutual advantage. It
is precisely on this basis that the USSR now renders economic and technical
assistance to many foreign states. . . .

We know that the government of Brazil, aiming to strengthen and advance
the national economy [so that it] would not depend on foreign monopoly
capital, worked out a 3-year plan for 1963-5 envisaging an annual 7%
increase in national production during this period. . . .

The Soviet government is ready to discuss economic cooperation with the
government of Brazil and to find mutually acceptable ways of promoting
Brazil's industrial development. An understanding could be reached, for
instance, on the deliveries of necessary machinery and equipment from the
USSR, on the dispatch of Soviet specialists to Brazil and on the training and
studies of Brazilian specialists in the USSR.

I think that the Soviet people, too, could borrow much that is useful from
what is being done in Brazil in construction and architecture, for instance. . . .

Silveira then asked—*Do you consider that the new forms
of social and economic organization in Cuba can produce positive results in spite of that country's isolation established by the
United States?* Khrushchev replied:

The U.S., having pledged not to invade Cuba, at the same time . . . does not
abandon its hostile policy towards the Cuban republic, its plans to destroy the
system existing on Cuba and to restore the rule of American monopolies.
Pressure is being exerted on the governments of other countries to make
them stop trading with Cuba [and] to break diplomatic, economic and other
relations. Recently, the U.S. government took new measures aimed at
restricting Cuba's trade with other countries. . . .

In other words, some [persons] in the U.S. are trying to isolate Cuba internationally—especially [from] Latin America. Moreover, the most aggressive
American circles, the *madmen* as they are called in the U.S. itself, are now
prodding the U.S. government to start on the criminal and treacherous road
[towards] armed invasion of Cuba. They say that the existence of a
differently-minded neighbor cannot be tolerated, that Cuba allegedly creates
a threat to the U.S. . . .

If a big state is permitted to impose its will on a small country by force, to
try to strangle it because that country's policy or social system does not suit
the imperialist monopolies, then today Cuba, tomorrow some other, and the
day after tomorrow a 3d Latin American country would fall victim to
iniquity and violence in international affairs. . . .

Cuba is not alone in her just struggle.... I am in a position to declare once more that the Soviet Union was and remains a loyal friend of revolutionary Cuba. We have given an assurance to the Cuban people that they can always count on our assistance and support. We shall not leave our Cuban friends in the lurch.

Silveira asked—*What influence, in your opinion, could be exerted by Latin American countries, particularly Brazil, on the solution of the most important international problems of our time?* Khrushchev replied:

... One can only welcome the efforts of the president of Brazil, Mr. Goulart, [the efforts] of the Brazilian government, in the struggle for normalizing international relations....

Brazil's active manifestations [in the quest] for a solution of disputed problems through negotiation, for general and complete disarmament, for a nuclear test ban are an important contribution to the relaxation of international tension. Brazil's positive role in the proceedings of the 18-nation Disarmament Committee is well known. The Soviet Union, as you know, supported the proposal of Brazil, Mexico and [6] other nonaligned countries in that committee [toward] facilitating agreement on ending all kind[s] of nuclear weapons tests.

The National Congress of Mexico recently appealed to parliamentarians of all countries to come out in favor of peace, general and complete disarmament and [a] ban on nuclear tests for military purposes.... We highly appreciate such steps by the Latin American countries, reflecting a sober approach to the major problem of our time—disarmament.... Of course, one cannot expect that the imperialists, the militarists themselves want to disarm. The aggressive circles in the West are doing and will do everything to frustrate the cause of disarmament....

Silveira's next question elicited Khrushchev's most extensive reply. Silveira asked—*What is your opinion of the European Common Market and its effect on the economy of countries of other continents that are traditional suppliers of raw materials?* Khrushchev said:

The European Common Market arose as a result of fierce rivalry between the imperialist powers. One of the principal trends of its activity is the economic and political struggle against the countries of the Socialist camp and also the countries of Asia, Africa and Latin America.

As for the European Common Market's effect on the state of international economic relations, it can be qualified as harmful and detrimental to normal economic relations.

The Soviet Union is consistently striving for the development of international trade and economic cooperation on an equal and mutually advantageous basis, without discrimination and artificial barriers.... The European Economic Community is carrying through its policy in quite a different direction. This determines our negative attitude to[wards] the European Common Market....

According to economists' most conservative estimates, the Latin American countries are annually losing some $1½ billion because of the gap in prices between industrial goods and raw materials.

Evidently, this is well understood in the Latin American countries themselves. The Brazilian delegate at the session of the UN General Assembly last September, speaking of the fatal consequences of nonequivalent prices, remarked that the Latin American countries "anxiously regard the fact that in the last 10 years foreign aid rendered to our continent was much less than the losses we sustained as a result of the drop in the prices of our products in the world market."

The Soviet Union considers it necessary to develop the struggle for the liquidation of this injustice. The Soviet Union is against restricted groups' hampering international trade....

(A 1963-5 Brazilian-USSR trade agreement was signed in Rio de Janeiro Apr. 20. Finance Min. Francisco San Tiago Dantas said he expected Brazilian-USSR trade to rise from a $70 million total in 1962 to $160 million in 1963, $200 million in 1964 and $220 million in 1965. Under the agreement, the USSR was to export to Brazil $35 million worth of such items as oil-drilling, mining and electronic equipment, planes, tractors, trucks, fertilizers, chemicals and medical instruments. Brazil was to export to the USSR such manufactured goods as musical instruments, films and fruit juices.)

Lobster Quarrel

The Brazilian navy Jan. 30 halted 3 Breton lobster boats operating off Recife and charged them with fishing illegally. Brazilian warships escorted the French vessels to the Brazilian port of Natal, where the resident French consul lodged a protest. The boats were released and permitted to continue their expedition unmolested after an exchange of messages by Pres. Goulart and French Pres. Charles de Gaulle.

Brazilian authorities had claimed in 1962 that Brazil's political and economic control extended below sea level as far as the rim of the continental shelf, 60 to 100 miles beyond the coast of Brazil. They argued that, since lobsters crawling along the continental shelf within those latitudes were on Brazilian territory, only Brazilian nationals were legally entitled to take them.

France, in July 1962, had proposed arbitration, but Brazil had rejected the suggestion. The French renewed this proposal as a demand Feb. 22, 1963.

The dispute had flared up again Feb. 19 when Brazil gave the French boats 48 hours to withdraw beyond the continental shelf. France Feb. 22 dispatched the frigate *Tartu* to protect the lobster boats. The Brazilian embassy in Paris protested to the French Foreign Ministry against the French naval move. Brazil Feb. 22 sent 2 destroyers to enforce its interpretation of the law on maritime rights.

Goulart and de Gaulle again exchanged messages, with Goulart saying Brazil would not negotiate until the French fishing boats and any naval support vessel had left the area. De Gaulle replied that the *Tartu* would continue on its mission to protect the Breton fishermen.

The Brazilian navy went on a state of alert Feb. 25. The *Tartu* was sighted about 90 miles off the northeast coast. Discussions began in Rio de Janeiro among Goulart, Foreign Min. Hermes Lima and the war, naval and air ministers. The Brazilian Foreign Ministry Feb. 27 issued an opinion asserting that negotiations between France and Brazil could make no headway until the *Tartu* withdrew.

France called the *Tartu* back before the month's end. Lima and French Amb.-to-Brazil Jacques Baeyens discussed the situation in Rio de Janeiro Mar. 1. The *N.Y. Times* reported Mar. 2 that Brazil had sent out warships and planes toward the French lobster boats. It reported Mar. 4 that France had dispatched the sloop *Paul-Goffeny* to replace the *Tartu* on duty off Brazil.

But in a statement issued at the Quai d'Orsay Mar. 8, the French Foreign Ministry announced that France had ordered the lobster boats to return to their home ports and had called back the *Paul-Goffeny*. France took the dispute to the International Bureau of the Permanent Court of Arbitration in The Hague Apr. 2 and asked the court to assert its jurisdiction in the matter.

Anzoategui Incident

Brazil became involved briefly in February in the Communist rebellion against Pres. Romulo Betancourt of Venezuela. The involvement was involuntary, and Brazil hewed closely to international law, being careful to maintain correct relations with its northern neighbor.

The affair began when 9 members of the Venezuelan anti-government Armed Forces National Liberation (FALN) Feb. 11 seized the 3,127-ton Venezuelan freighter *Anzoategui* 70 miles off the Venezuelan coast. The rebels, whose organization was pro-Castro and pro-Communist, eluded an international sea and air search and finally anchored the ship Feb. 17 in Brazilian territorial waters near the island of Maraca (240 miles north of Belem). Brazilian marines then boarded the vessel and took it into custody. The 9 FALN men were taken off the ship Feb. 18 and brought to Rio de Janeiro Feb. 22 for hearings on their appeal for Brazilian asylum and a Venezuelan demand for their extradition.

The *Anzoategui* had left the Venezuelan port of La Guaira Feb. 11 for Houston and New Orleans. Later Feb. 11 8 FALN men, who had stowed away on the ship, were led by Wilmar Medina Rojas, the *Anzoategui*'s 2d mate and also an FALN member, in forcing Capt. Oscar Pereira and his 35-man crew at gunpoint point to surrender the ship. The rebels said they would hold the crew and captain as hostages for the release of political prisoners in Venezuela. Their main purpose, however, reportedly was to force Pres. Romulo Betancourt to cancel a projected visit to the U.S.

U.S. Navy ships and planes set out Feb. 12 in response to a Venezuelan appeal to help track down the *Anzoategui*. A U.S. Navy plane eventually spotted the vessel off Surinam. Planes gathered and fired 13 rockets across the ship's bow after transmitting a Navy order for the *Anzoategui* to change course to Puerto Rico. The rebels ignored the order and denounced the rocket firing as a violation of international law and "an abuse of Venezuela's national sovereignty." (U.S. officials in Washington said that the Navy had acted in response to a rebel request for possible U.S. asylum.)

Venezuelan Foreign Min. Marcos Falcon Briceno had asserted beforehand that his government considered the ship's seizure an act of piracy. He had also said that "the mutinous crewmen may be tried under the international piracy law by any country that captures them." The Cuban government, however, reportedly offered the hijackers political asylum if they managed to make a Cuban port.

Brazilian authorities disregarded a Venezuelan appeal to bar the *Anzoategui* from its territorial waters. Subsequently, however, they returned the vessel to its owners, the Venezuelan Navigation Co., and repatriated to Venezuela, at their own request, the captain and the rest of the crew.

Tito in Brazil

Yugoslav Pres. Tito, 71, arrived in Brasilia Sept. 18 on the first leg of a 4-country Latin American tour that also included Peru, Chile and Mexico. The purpose of Tito's Latin American tour was to appeal for closer trade relations and to seek support for his policy of non-alignment. His accompanying party included his wife, Foreign Min. Koca Popovic and Parliament Vice Pres. Mijalko Todorovic.

Tito, greeted in Brasilia by Pres. Goulart, was forced to confine his entire 5-day Brazilian visit to Brasilia because right-wing Govs. Carlos Lacerda of Guanabara State and Ademar de Barros of Sao Paulo State had refused to extend official greetings to him in the states' principal cities of Rio de Janeiro and Sao Paulo. The Roman Catholic Church, led by Jaime Cardinal de Barros Camara, archbishop of Rio de Janeiro, also denounced Tito's visit.

Brazil Host to 'Alliance' Conference

The 2d annual review meeting of the Alliance for Progress was held in Sao Paulo, Brazil Nov. 11-16. The conference, attended by delegates from the U.S. and 19 Latin American countries, was sponsored by the Economic & Social Council of the Organization of American States. Brazilian Finance Min. Carlos Carvalho Pinto was elected conference president.

In a speech opening the talks Nov. 11, Brazilian Pres. Joao Goulart questioned the ability of the U.S. aid program to solve Latin America's economic problems. He said that restrictive trade barriers "represent a continual bleeding of our economies." Goulart asserted that "palliatives or false, superficial concessions" by industrialized exporting nations were not the answer to "breaking" Latin America's "agrarian structure..., in which the barriers of feudalism and intolerable privileges suffocate our effort for development, industrialization and diversification." Goulart urged the "establishment of a new international division of labor, just and remunerative prices for our exports of raw materials, expansion of our exports of manufactures and semi-manufactures."

The creation of an Inter-American Committee of the Alliance for Progress (ICAP) was approved at the final meeting Nov. 16 by 19-1 vote. The committee, first proposed at a pre-conference meeting Nov. 8, would be empowered to recommend financial and other measures within the Alliance program and measures for policing its operations. Actual control of the funds, however, would remain under U.S. jurisdiction. Brazil voted reluctantly for ICAP because it regarded its scope as too limited. In deference to Brazil's objections, the conference agreed to instruct ICAP to present, 6 months after its establishment, a report on an Alliance development fund as proposed by Brazil.

Legislators Shot to Death

Journalists had begun using such terms as "wide-open" to describe the social and political climate in some regions of Brazil after the fatal gun duel between members of feuding factions Sept. 13, 1957 inside the Alagoas State legislature in Maceio.

The next instance of such conduct came Aug. 31 when Rio Grande do Sul Assemblyman Euclides Kleimann, a Social Democrat, was shot to death while broadcasting his part in a continuing political debate over a radio station in Santa Cruz do Sul, a city of about 9,500 people 80 miles west of Porto Alegre. (Porto Alegre police had not yet solved the violent death of his wife, Margit, in 1962.)

The Associated Press reported the arrest of City Councilman Floriano Peixoto, a Brazilian Laborite, who, the police said, had burst into the studio, drawn a pistol and killed Kleimann instantly. Radio listeners could hear shouting before the gunfire. According to the AP account, both men had received equal-time allotments on the radio—"each to alternate a day on the air"—in a statewide election campaign slated to end in November. The campaign had been marked by great bitterness between the 2 men and their political parties.

(The state's Social Democratic organization, disavowing the former national alliance [PSD-PTB] with the Brazilian Laborites, had earlier joined forces with the PTB's chief opponents, the National Democratic Union [UDN]. In the 1962 gubernatorial election, Ildo Meneghetti, the PSD-UDN candidate and a former governor, had defeated Egydio Michaelsen, the PTB candidate, despite the support for Michaelsen of Leonel Brizola, the outgoing governor.)

Sen. Jose Cairala of Acre State was fatally wounded Dec. 4 in a gunfight that erupted on the floor of the Senate in Brasilia between 2 other Senators, both from the minute northeastern state of Alagoas. Cairala died the same day in a nearby hospital after emergency surgery for the removal of a bullet from his abdomen.

The *N.Y. Times* reported Dec. 5 that at least 4 shots had been exchanged by Sens. Armon de Melo, a Christian Democrat, and Silvestre Pericles, a Brazilian Laborite, as de Melo took the rostrum to address the Senate. Pericles had said he would kill de Melo if he spoke before the Senate on matters relating to Alagoas State, where the 2 were bitter rivals. The session was suspended and both Senators were taken into custody by Senate guards; they were deprived Dec. 7 of their Congressional immunity from arrest.

1964

GOULART'S DOWNFALL

The Goulart administration lasted 2½ years. It was overthrown Mar. 31-Apr. 2 in a military and civil rebellion that lasted about 48 hours and achieved, with relatively little bloodshed, the collapse of all effective resistance. The revolt ushered in, however, a period of military predominance in Brazil's political affairs.

Goulart's Last New Year's Message

Pres. Joao Goulart opened the year traditionally by delivering a New Year's message to the Brazilian people. Reviewing the events of 1963, Goulart said Jan. 2 that peace and domestic liberty had been maintained. He admitted, however, that the year had been full of difficulties: economic growth in 1963, for one thing, had not been satisfactory.

Goulart asserted that many of Brazil's hardships were caused by international factors. He added that the country could not pay that portion of its foreign debt coming due by the end of 1965—some $350 million—without a further slowing of Brazil's economic development rate. He said that the government would shortly appeal to the country's creditors for permission to delay payment.

The president declared in closing that the country needed such radical changes as land and electoral reform. Armed forces enlisted personnel and illiterates, too, should be permitted to vote, Goulart declared, and Brazil's poor smallholders should receive the opportunity to own and work a greater share of the land.

Labor Unrest: Higher Wages Demanded

During the first half of January oil workers downed tools in Bahia, merchant seamen and gasworks employes walked off the job in Rio de Janeiro and interurban telephone operators left their switchboards. Most of the workers on strike demanded wage and salary increases of 100% to keep up with the galloping inflation. Government employes, too, continued to press wage demands. They called for an extra month's salary as a Christmas bonus, a benefit already received by employes of private industry.

Goulart Feb. 22 signed into law new and higher minimum-wage schedules at a mass rally organized by the General Workers' Command (CGT) in Rio de Janeiro. The new law doubled wages in Guanabara, Brasilia, Sao Paulo and Belo Horizonte, where a worker's monthly pay previously averaged 42,000 cruzeiros.

Public-Domain Decree Delayed

Joao Pinheiro Neto, director of the agrarian reform program, submitted to Goulart in mid-January a decree for the expropriation of all lands within 10 kilometers (6¼ miles) of federal roads, railways and reservoirs.

Pinheiro Neto, continuing the pressure for his program's acceptance by Congress, revised this section to exclude: (a) urban and suburban areas; (b) properties of less than 100 hectares (247 acres) or land containing villages or small towns; (c) land exploited to a degree not below the average for the region; (d) land used for industrial purposes, for mining or as a site for dam and power stations authorized by the government, and (e) land belonging to public authorities. Land not in any of these categories also would be excluded if rented within 180 days to workers' cooperatives for at least 5 years.

Goulart, however, did not sign the decree at once but delayed in order that he might confer with and hear the complaints of various state governors opposed to the legislation.

Rumors started circulating throughout Brazil in mid-February that landless farm workers had begun organizing in preparation for taking over landed estates and plantations in the country's interior when the land-reform legislation became law. Radio Globo of Rio de Janeiro Feb. 18 broadcast reports that landowners in the state of Goias had countered such a contingency by organizing for the armed defense of their lands. Radio Tupi of Rio de Janeiro reported Feb. 18 that, in the state of Minas Gerais, members of the Rural Association of Land-owners were preparing to defend their farms.

Foreign Remittances Curbed

Goulart Jan. 17 signed a decree that finally put into operation Law No. 4131 of Sept. 3, 1962, limiting most profit remittances abroad annually by foreign investors to 10% of their Brazilian capitalization. All foreign firms already had to register the amount of their total investment in the country. (By July 1963, more than 12,000 business entities had begun such reports.)

Goulart, signing the bill amid rumors of revolution, said: "Those who accuse me are the same ones who brought about conditions that resulted in the overthrow of [Getulio] Vargas." He also cited the late U.S. Pres. John F. Kennedy's famous alternatives of either "reform or revolution" in justifying the need for the law.

(Marshal Osvino Ferreira Alves, former commander of the First Army, assumed office Jan. 28 as president of Petrobras, the state oil monopoly.)

Sailors & Marines Screen Potemkin Mutiny Film

Brazilian marine corps enlisted men Feb. 13 attended a showing of *The Battleship Potemkin*. This Soviet-made silent film by Sergei M. Eisenstein was about a famous incident in the Russian imperial navy in 1905: sailors took over a vessel of the

Black Sea fleet and brought it to port in Odessa; the leaders of the mutiny were then arrested and executed. The film was shown under the auspices of Cpl. Jose Anselmo Duarte's left-wing Sailors & Marines Association.

Moderate Leftist Grouping Fails

Pres. Goulart failed in February in his attempt to knit together a moderate left-of-center political coalition, called the *Frente Unica* (Single Front), to rival his brother-in-law Leonel Brizola's militant leftist *Frente de Mobilizacao Popular* (Popular Mobilization Front).

Goulart had sought to have Deputy Francisco San Tiago Dantas of Minas Gerais, the ex-finance minister, and Gov. Miguel Arraes of Pernambuco State lead the alliance. Too much suspicion of Goulart existed among moderates of both the left and the right, however, for them to unite around him. The president's aim in forming such a grouping apparently had been to collect enough Congressional and countrywide support to ensure the enactment of his program of social reforms.

Political and social tension increased in Belo Horizonte, capital of Minas Gerais State, when Brizola's Popular Mobilization Front staged a mass meeting Feb. 25 to rally support for ultranationalist reforms. Deputy Brizola, protected by marine corps enlisted men, was prevented by political opponents from delivering a prepared speech and was forced to leave the auditorium.

Goulart Overthrown

A series of events beginning Friday, Mar. 13, with a public rally in Rio de Janeiro built into an army revolt Mar. 31 and ended Apr. 2 with the overthrow of Pres. Joao Goulart's administration.

For the 2d time within 9 years a Brazilian chief executive was forcefully prevented from finishing his term of office. As in 1955-6, an effort was made to observe constitutional amenities after the coup. This time, however, there was an even stronger reluctance on the part of the ousted president to leave his office during a term that still had 22 months to run.

The forces overthrowing Goulart had foreseen most contingencies and succeeded in carrying out his removal and suppressing all resistance. In less than 2 weeks they strengthened the executive power greatly through a decree substantially altering the 1946 constitution.

The Mar. 13 rally—of Goulart's supporters—took place in the *praca* (square) before the big railroad station in Rio de Janeiro. The aim of the convocation was to mobilize public opinion in behalf of the social reforms that Goulart claimed Brazil needed urgently.

More than 123,000 people (including the soldiers present) thronged the *praca* at the rally and flaunted banners with slogans in support of Goulart or demanding the legalization of the long-outlawed Communist Party. Prominent public figures who sat behind the speakers' platform included: War Min. Jair Dantas Ribeiro, Justice Min. Abelardo Jurema, Gov. Miguel Arraes of Pernambuco and Gov. Badger Silveira of Rio de Janeiro. Before Pres. and Mrs. Goulart arrived, Deputy Leonel Brizola of Guanabara attacked Congress as no longer representative of the people.

Goulart appeared about 3 hours after the start of the rally. He held up dramatically, before the cheering throng, decrees he had just signed. The decrees put public-domain expropriation orders into immediate effect and transferred Brazil's 6 privately owned oil refineries to the control of Petrobras. Goulart also announced at the rally that the next day—Mar. 14—he would sign a decree imposing rent controls. Goulart spoke for a little more than an hour. He called for constitutional changes to overhaul what he called the current "outmoded" regime. Goulart said: "It is time to reform structures, methods, ways of working and objectives."

The promised constitutional amendments were formally requested by Goulart in an annual message submitted to Congress Mar. 15. Among his proposals: payment for expropriated property in government bonds instead of cash; suffrage for illiterates and the armed forces privates and noncommissioned officers. Goulart said the amendments would "contribute to the freeing of national energies crushed by the narrowness of an outdated economic structure that serves the interests of privileged groups only." Goulart warned that unless the reforms were effected, "bloody convulsion" would result. (It was reported that Goulart's opponents and some of his supporters feared that he also was planning to seek a constitutional change that would permit him to succeed himself after his current term expired in 1966.)

Some 500,000 citizens of Sao Paulo took part Mar. 19 in a demonstration of protest against Goulart's social-reform moves and policies. The "March of the Family with God for Liberty," supported by the local hierarchy, converged on the *Praca da Republica,* where ex-Pres. Eurico Gaspar Dutra urged support of the 1946 constitution and declared himself against Goulart's appeals to amend it. (Other speakers demanded the arrest of Leonel Brizola.)

The Social Democratic Party (PSD) Mar. 20 nominated ex-Pres. Juscelino Kubitschek, a Senator from Goias State, to be the party's candidate again for president. The delegates at the PSD convention gave 2,826 votes to Kubitschek and one to ex-Pres. Dutra; 39 delegates abstained.

Brazil's chief of staff, Gen. Humberto de Alencar Castelo Branco, sent a secret memo warning the top-ranking officers in the army (the general staff of the War Ministry) Mar. 20 of the dangerous political situation that had developed. The memo said:

> I understand the worry and concern among my subordinates in the days following the political rally of Mar. 13. I realize that they are found not only among the general staff of the army and in dependent sectors, but also among the troops, in other organizations, and in the 2 other military services. I participated in them, and they were the reason for my conference with the war minister.
>
> 2 threats are evident: the advent of a Constituent Assembly as a means for achieving basic reforms and the unleashing on a large scale of agitations generalized from the illegal power of the General Workers' Command [CGT]. The armed forces were called on to support such objectives.
>
> In order to understand the problem some preliminary considerations are necessary: The national and permanent military role is not properly to defend the government's programs, much less its propaganda, but to guarantee the constitutional powers, their functioning, and the enforcement of laws. The armed forces were not established to proclaim their solidarity with one power or another. If the option to stand behind programs, political movements or holders of high offices was permitted them, then necessarily there would be the right also of opposition. Relative to the doctrine that admits their use as a pressure force against one of the [constitutional] powers it is logical that it also would be admissible to turn them against any one of them. Not being a militia, the armed forces are not weapons for anti-democratic support. They are to guarantee the constructional authorities and the coexistence of the constitutional powers.

The ambitious Constituent Assembly is a violent revolutionary objective for the closing of the present Congress and the institution of a dictatorship.

Insurrection is a legitimate recourse for a people. It can be asked: Are the Brazilian people requesting a military dictatorship or a civilian dictatorship and a Constituent Assembly? Not yet, it would appear.

Will the armed forces enter into a revolution to deliver Brazil to a group that wishes to dominate it in order to command and countermand just to enjoy power; in order to guarantee full power to a pseudo-syndicated group whose leaders live on subversive action each time more onerous for the public coffers; in order perhaps to submit the nation to Moscow communism? This certainly would be antipatriotic, antinational and antipopular.

No. The armed forces cannot betray Brazil. To defend the privileges of the wealthy is in the same antidemocratic direction as serving fascist dictatorships or syndicalist communists.

The CGT announced that it will support the paralyzing of the country as a revolutionary scheme. A public calamity probably will occur. And there are those who desire that the armed forces remain outside of or servile to subversive orders.

The duty of the armed forces is neither one nor the other. It is to guarantee the enforcement of the law, not allowing an illegal movement of such gravity for the life of the nation.

I have been dealing with the political situation to characterize our military conduct.

The armed forces have acted legally and have also exhibited a high understanding in view of the difficulty and deviations inherent in the present stage of Brazilian evolution. And they have remained, as is their duty, loyal to the professional life, to their destination and, with continuing respect to their leaders, to the authority of the president of the republic.

It is necessary here to stay always within the limits of the law; to be ready to defend legality; to be aware through the integral functioning of the 3 constitutional branches and through the enforcement of laws, including those that ensure the electoral process; and to be against revolution for dictatorship and a Constituent Assembly, against the CGT and against discrediting the historic role of the armed forces.

The most worthy war minister has declared that he will assure respect for Congress, elections and the inauguration of the elected candidate. He has, furthermore, declared that there will be no military pressure exerted on Congress.

This is what I have to say in consideration of the worry and inquiries deriving from the present political situation and with respect to the current military conduct.

The army uprising against Goulart took place Mar. 31. The immediate cause of the revolt was a short-lived mutiny by 1,425 pro-Goulart sailors and marines in Rio de Janeiro Mar. 25. The mutineers, members of the left-wing Sailors & Marines Association, seized the Metallurgical Workers Union building after holding a meeting there in protest against the arrest earlier Mar. 25 of Cpl. Jose Anselmo Duarte, the association's president, and of 11 directors and about 30 members. Duarte and the others had been charged with insubordination after Duarte called for support of Goulart's reform program and denounced "reactionary authorities protected by archaic regulations and unconstitutional decrees." Goulart and Adm. Candido Aragao, marine commander, had been invited by the association to attend the meeting, but they refused.

Adm. Silvio Mota, the navy minister, called on the rebels to leave the building and submit to arrest. The rebels refused. Instead, they seized the building.

Mota resigned his post Mar. 26; he was said to have felt that Goulart did not support his efforts to suppress the association. Before resigning, Mota dismissed Adm. Aragao as marine commander and appointed Rear Adm. Luis Felipe Sinai as his successor. Aragao was later reinstated. (Goulart accepted Mota's resignation Mar. 27 and appointed Adm. Paulo Maria da Cunha Rodrigues as navy minister.)

A navy communique issued Mar. 26 denounced the mutineers and charged that "they allege false claims which are not among the aims of our progressive navy."

The mutineers surrendered to army troops Mar. 27 following a plea from Goulart but only after a threatened clash between the association members and their captors. One truckload of mutineers who had been taken to the Navy Ministry escaped and ran back to the union building after labor officials charged that they were being led into a trap. The mutineers finally gave up after the army warned that it would attack their stronghold. The sailors and marines were later released for duty. The government—in an action later reversed—granted the mutineers' demands for amnesty and recognition of their association. (The amnesty also applied to navy and air force personnel who had participated in a one-day revolt in Brasilia in Sept. 1963.)

A group of about 2,000 naval officers met in Rio de Janeiro Mar. 28 and accused the Goulart regime of undermining military discipline by failing to punish the navy and marine mutineers. A 2d pronouncement issued by the naval officers Mar. 29 called on the country to oppose "communization." The officers had urged Adm. Rodrigues, the new navy minister, to punish the mutineers and to dismiss Aragao.

Goulart Mar. 30 ordered an inquiry into the decision to grant the mutineers amnesty. He also called for an investigation of the Mar. 28 and 29 naval officers' meetings and of an incident in which the mutineers, on their release, staged a parade. In the procession, the sailors and marines carried on their shoulders in triumph Aragao and Adm. Pedro Suzano, chief of staff. As a result of the probe, the amnesty decree was rescinded.

Goulart later Mar. 30 declared in a nationwide TV broadcast that he would continue to seek economic reforms despite opposition to the program by his political enemies. He charged that this opposition was "financed by illicit remittances by big foreign companies [drug manufacturers and petroleum companies]" and landowners.

The army revolt followed Mar. 31 and ended in Goulart's downfall. The military acted against Goulart because of what military leaders considered his pro-Communist sympathies. The uprising started in the state of Minas Gerais and quickly spread to other parts of the country.

The army rebellion was first announced Mar. 31 by Gen. Olimpio Mourao, commander of the 4th Military Region in the Minas Gerais city of Juiz de Fora. In a radio proclamation, Mourao declared the city to be the "revolutionary capital of Brazil" and gave these reasons for the anti-Goulart revolt: "For more than 2 years, the enemies of order and democracy, shielded by the impunity given by the president, have been acting without respect for the institutions, scorning the armed forces and weakening the respect due to the public authorities.... Political unions maneuvered by Brazil's enemies, confessed Communists, have become more audacious under the president's stimulation, and ... they speak in the name of a foreign state whose imperialist interests they serve as subversive criminals to betray the Brazilian nation. The present government ... has been serving those labor organizations, giving them official and semi-official support, even giving them power to hire and fire ministers, generals and high officials, seeking this way to undermine true democratic institutions...."

The rebels were quickly joined by Maj. Gen. Amaury Kruel, one of Goulart's most valued supporters in the succession crisis of Aug.-Sept. 1961 and currently the commander of the 2d Army (based in Sao Paulo), by scattered army units in other parts of Brazil, by a number of admirals and generals and by the administrations of 8 of Brazil's 27 states and territories. Among those who lined up with the insurgents was Guanabara State Gov. Carlos Lacerda, an anti-Communist and long-time political foe of Goulart. Goulart retained the support of the 3d Army, commanded by Gen. Ladario Pereira Teles in Rio Grande do Sul State; Teles assumed control of the state's militia.

Gen. Jair Dantas Ribeiro, who was in a Rio de Janeiro hospital recovering from an operation, resigned as war minister as he realized he was losing control of the army.

The pro-Goulart, left-wing General Confederation of Workers Mar. 31 carried out its threat to strike the railroads to block any attempt to oust Goulart. Some railroad service was tied up by the walkout. The union also called a general strike in Rio de Janeiro, crippling transportation and food distribution.

Deputy Leonel Brizola, Goulart's brother-in-law, announced in a broadcast in Porto Alegre (capital of Rio Grande do Sul) that he had taken responsibility for the military defense of Goulart's regime.

The rebels arrested several high-ranking government officials. Among those seized: Justice Min. Abelardo Jurema, as he was about to leave Rio de Janeiro by plane; Rio de Janeiro State Gov. Badger Silveira; Pernambuco State Gov. Miguel Arraes in Recife, the capital. One student was killed in Recife in a clash between leftist and non-leftist students.

The rebels announced Apr. 1 that Goulart had resigned and had been replaced as president by Chamber of Deputies Pres. Ranieri Mazzili, next in line of succession. But Goulart, who fled Rio de Janeiro by plane Apr. 1, denied on arriving in Brasilia that he had resigned. Expressing determination to retain office, Goulart declared: "My mandate is untouchable. I will defend it until I die. There is no end to the situation yet. The rebel would-be coup makers have not yet dominated the situation."

Goulart, belying reports that he would go before Congress and declare martial law, emplaned Apr. 2 and flew from Brasilia to Porto Alegre, capital of his home state of Rio Grande do Sul—apparently in search of support from 3d Army units there. When the army instead occupied the state capital, Goulart abandoned further resistance and crossed with his family into neighboring Uruguay, which extended to them political asylum.

Rebel Leaders Force Change in Constitution

The military, naval and air officers who led the successful rebellion presented Congress Apr. 7 with a demand for vastly enlarged executive powers with which to conduct a sweeping "decommunization" program. Although Congress balked, the demanded powers were made law Apr. 9 in an Institutional Act *(Ato Institucional)* promulgated by the 3 new service ministers—Gen. Artur da Costa e Silva (for war), Adm. Augusto Rademaker (navy) and Brig. Francisco Correia de Melo (air)—who called themselves the Supreme Military Revolutionary Command.

The Institutional Act decreed that:

(1) The existing federal and state constitutions would be maintained, with the modifications introduced by the *Ato Institucional.*

(2) The election of the president and vice president of the republic to serve for the remainder of the current presidential term would be conducted by Congress within 2 days of the publication of the *Ato Institucional.*

(3) The president of the republic could send to Congress proposals for the 1946 constitution's amendment. These proposals would have to be considered within 30 days, with a 2d session after a minimum interval of 10 days; the proposals would be considered approved if they received an absolute majority in both houses in both sessions.

(4) The president could send to Congress bills on any matter, and they must be considered within 30 days by the deputies and within a like period by the Senate. Should the bills not be so considered, they would be deemed to have been approved.

(5) The right to introduce bills creating or increasing public expenditure would be reserved to the president. No Congressional amendment increasing the expenditure proposed by the president would be permitted.

(6) The president could, in any of the instances foreseen in the constitution, decree a state of siege, or prolong one, for a maximum of 30 days.

(7) All guarantees of *vitaliciedade e estabilidade* (life tenure and stability in office), whether constitutional or legal, were suspended for 6 months; office holders could, after summary investigation, be (by decree) dismissed, suspended, retired or transferred to the reserve. This article also affected state and municipal public servants.

(8) Investigations and legal processes with regard to crimes against the state or its property, as well as against the political and social order, could be initiated either against individuals or collectively.

(9) The commanders-in-chief could suspend political rights for a period of 10 months and annul legislative mandates (federal, state or municipal) without judicial review. This right would pass within 60 days to the president, who would act on the recommendations of the National Security Council.

(10) The *Ato Institucional* would remain in effect from the date of its signing until Jan. 31, 1966.

Castelo Branco Made President

The rebellion's military leaders won from state governors supporting them agreement that the victorious authorities should tender Pres. Goulart's unexpired term of office to Gen. Humberto de Alencar Castelo Branco, 63, the army chief of staff and apparent mastermind of the revolt.

The Senate and Chamber of Deputies convened Apr. 11 in joint session and chose Castelo Branco as Brazil's new chief executive. With 72 Brazilian Labor Party members abstaining, the vote was 361 in favor of Castelo Branco and 5 written-in ballots for 2 undeclared candidates. Jose Maria Alkmim, ex-Pres. Kubitschek's finance minister, became vice president.

INDEX